THE CRESTLINE SERIES

BIG RIGS | OF THE 1950s

THE CRESTLINE SERIES

BIG RIGS OF THE 1950s

RON ADAMS

MBI

First published in 2001 by MBI, an imprint of MBI Publishing Company, Galtier Plaza, Suite 200, 380 Jackson Street, St. Paul, MN 55101-3885 USA

The information in this book is true and complete to the best of our knowledge. All recommendations are made without any guarantee on the part of the author or Publisher, who also disclaim any liability incurred in connection with the use of this data or specific details.

This publication has been prepared solely by MBI Publishing Company and is not approved or licensed by any other entity. We recognize that some words, model names, and designations mentioned herein are the property of the trademark holder. We use them for identification purposes only. This is not an official publication.

MBI titles are also available at discounts in bulk quantity for industrial or sales-promotional use. For details write to Special Sales Manager at MBI Publishing Company, Galtier Plaza, Suite 200, 380 Jackson Street, St. Paul, MN 55101-3885 USA

Library of Congress Cataloging-in-Publication Data
Adams, Ronald.
    Big rigs of the 1950s / Ronald Adams.
        p. cm. — (The Crestline series)
    Includes index.
    ISBN-13: 978-0-7603-0978-0
    ISBN-10: 0-7603-0978-7 (pbk. : alk. paper)
        1. Tractor trailer combinations—History. I. Title. II. Series.

TL230.5.T73 A33   2001
629.224'09'045—dc21   20011030593

On the front cover:

Top left: Shown carrying more than 22,000 bottles of soda for the Coca Cola Co. on its Trailmobile trailer is this Autocar U Model, which came in a tractor version. *A.T.H.S. Zoe James Library*

Top right: This White WC-24 tractor and Fruehauf trailer appears to have been going to Roadway Express Inc. of Akron, Ohio. *White Motor Co.*

Bottom left: The D Series was the fourth cab-over-engine model in the Mack line-up. This particular model was the low version, which was used mostly for local delivery work. This D-42 was set up as a tractor for the Houston Steel Drum Co. Inc. of Houston, Texas, in 1955. *Mack Trucks*

Bottom right: Kenworth introduced the the cab-beside-engine (CBE) model in 1953. It was available in a day cab or with a sleeper berth behind the driver and the engine. Weight was reduced by eliminating the right top half of the cab. From the looks of it, this one was joining the fleet of the Denver Chicago Trucking Co., Inc. *Kenworth*

On the back cover:

Top: This circa-1951-52 model Peterbilt truck-trailer combination was owned by Capitol Tank Lines Inc., a California-based tanker hauler. Notice that the turn signals at this time were still the cab mounted swing-out type. *Ron Adams Collection*

Bottom: Brockway's 158 Cargo model is shown here being used by Marr Scaffolding Co. of South Boston, Massachusetts. *Brockway*

Edited by Steve Hendrickson
Designed by Two Poppie's Design

Printed in Hong Kong

— Contents —

Dedication

To do a book such as this was fun and as big a challenge for me as driving these trucks was for drivers in the 1950s. The drivers who braved going out in all kinds of weather. The drivers who tired themselves out shifting gears trying to conquer those long hard grades and mountains. The drivers who repaired their own trucks in all kinds of conditions. The drivers who had to load and unload their own trucks. The drivers who took a break at some diner for a cup of coffee and a piece of delicious good old apple pie. The drivers who made the steering wheel and the seat their bed when no sleeper was available. The drivers who had humorous times when a bunch of them got together in the drivers' bunk rooms.

These were the guys who gave us those long lines of traffic going up those long grades on those two-lane highways. These were the guys who drove those trucks that made the noise that you could hear a mile away. These were the guys who were dedicated to their job of getting their rigs from here to there and back again. These were the guys who wore a chauffeur's cap, a chained wallet, and a patch on their shirt that showed the name of the company they drove for, and wore it proudly; the guys who would stop to help a stranded motorist or a fellow trucker. Yes, they did it all. So to all those "truck drivin' men" who drove those "Big Rigs" across America's highways, I dedicate this to you.

Acknowledgments

I would like to take this opportunity to thank everyone who was responsible for sending me the photographs and pictures that I used in this book. The photo credits for each picture are the people and sources that made this book possible. It took many years to accumulate these photos, and some of the people who sent me these photos for trucking companies are probably no longer with us. So to those who are gone and to those of you who are still with us, a great big thank-you for your efforts and contributions for making this book a success.

—Ronald Adams

Introduction

For more than 100 years, America's railroads reigned supreme as the finest land transportation system in the world. There were tracks everywhere connecting the United States' cities and towns with the seaports and industrial centers. Railroads carried coal, grain, livestock, produce, and building materials, and they did it well. On-line cities and towns prospered as industries grew at trackside locations, and generally, the country grew up around the rail lines.

The railroads retained their strength through World War II, and even into the 1950s. But after the war, as millions of red-blooded American boys returned home from military service, a new era of transportation was about to be born. This is not to say that the trucking industry wasn't active before the war, but the situation would change rapidly.

Roads and highways had improved greatly since the first world war. No longer was the family car or the local trucker limited to service around town. People and parcels traveled from town to town, and even city to city, with increasing regularity.

Vehicles had improved vastly as well, a small positive benefit of the war itself. Literally millions of cars, trucks, engines, and machinery had been developed and built during the war. The diesel engine and the heavy truck had convincingly come of age, and the American trucking industry, in its rather puny prewar form, had been pressed into carrying sizes and volumes previously unimagined.

It was all a tremendous learning experience. Civilian truckers learned greatly from the feats and resulting accomplishments they had endured under the pressures of war. During that same period, millions of young men and women were entering the service, only to find that one of the largest facets of fighting a war was the element of transportation. Aside from the obvious shipping of men, women, and equipment overseas, millions of tons of supplies and materiel had to be moved over both land and sea. In most bombed-out countries, the existing rail lines were of little use. So where was all this stuff going to go? Over the roads, of course.

The Army Corps of Engineers and the Navy Seabees operated huge numbers of trucks, but all military branches were constantly involved in the business of supplying the forces with food, ammunition, medical supplies, and clothing. Also, as a matter of dire necessity, the American military forces became extremely proficient at building roads, airfields, bridges, docks, barracks and ammo and fuel depots, much of which had to be done in jig-time.

It has been said that for every fighting soldier, there are at least two people in supporting roles. And what were all of these people doing? Moving stuff! And, when it was over, a whole generation of people came home with a very different viewpoint as to how things could be done.

Many of the returning servicemen and servicewomen had gained experience in some form of transportation business, and many of them, experienced or not, would enter some form of transportation job in their civilian life. Few would be offered jobs with the railroads, because the railroads had experienced extensive layoffs since the beginning of the depression, and therefore most had a considerable backlog of manpower vying for the few postwar positions available.

The New Transportation Boom

In fact, two new transportation industries were about to bloom, as the airline industry would expand along with the trucking industry in the 1950s. Not coincidentally, the airlines' growth was also powered by people who had flown as pilots or crew, or worked as ground crew during the war and desired to pursue these professions as a career afterward.

It's likely that more new trucking companies were formed in the first five years following World War II than at any other time except the period following deregulation in the 1980s. In addition to the many new companies, old companies were revived with the transfusion of new talent trained in the war. Many would become dispatchers, dock men, rate clerks, salesmen, and terminal managers.

Many more would become truck drivers. In many cases, a few hundred dollars mustering-out pay provided the down payment on an old Ford or International. Surprisingly, many of these investments, and lots of hard work, resulted in the formation of many substantial trucking companies in the postwar era.

Business levels in the trucking industry doubled and quadrupled as shippers swung over from the railroads to the overnight, door-to-door services trucks provided. This new generation of truck-minded people had moved into all forms of industry, and more and more, the decision to use trucks instead of rail was made.

Simultaneously, Americans were taking to the road in droves. Car sales were climbing steadily. The need for better roads began as a murmur, and was ultimately sung as an anthem heard loud and clear by legislatures everywhere. The song was joined by shippers, builders, and most importantly, by consumers. This was a generation of busy people, devoid of the patience to wait for a railcar to be shunted through Peoria.

And so better roads were built, from simple widening and rebuilding programs to the construction of new toll roads that soared on for miles over ribbons of concrete. By the early 1950s, we had a New Jersey Turnpike and a New York State Thruway. But the real answer came in 1956 when President Eisenhower signed the Federal Highway Aid Bill into law, which would produce our Interstate Highway System. The building of this network would not only provide countless jobs and bolster industry, but most importantly, it would firmly establish the nation's over-the-road routes of commerce indefinitely.

Revamping Equipment

The trucking companies that operated through the war were mostly older companies, started during the prosperous 1920s or before, supplemented by late-1930s and early-1940s startups nurtured largely on the buildup preceding World War II.

The fleet of over-the-road trucks operating around the country before the war was made up largely of rather aged vehicles. By the time the real buildup began in 1940, many older trucking companies were enjoying their first real upswing in business since the depression. Very fortunate were those companies that could foresee enough profit margin to order and receive delivery on new equipment before the war began. By early 1942 the government put a complete stop to the production of civilian vehicles as the country committed completely to the war effort. A "make-do" attitude prevailed; nothing said it better than the defense slogan, "Keep-'em-rolling." Many folks will remember the familiar red-and-blue flag device with a large gold letter E on it that was awarded to companies who displayed particular efficiency in their operations, to make things last and reduce waste.

Many of the vehicles that should have been replaced a decade earlier were still running daily in 1945, and some would not see retirement until the early 1950s. Most noticeable was the lack of horsepower in the older trucks, as they held up traffic, crawling up hills with huge loads on the old single-lane roads. A prewar highway tractor probably had an average of 115 to 120 horsepower as opposed to about 150 to 160 in an early postwar model.

Common also in this period were the large straight trucks, 6 wheelers and 10 wheelers that were often used in highway transport operation. In many states, particularly in the Midwest and on the West Coast, it was common practice to hook a two- or three-axle trailer behind them, as size and weight laws often permitted this. It was not unusual for one of these large combination units to gross close to 72,000 pounds and have no more than 110 horsepower under the hood. True, some of the big, old truck engines had the wall-climbing torque to pull the load, but horsepower is the factor we must consider when examining how fast it will pull it.

In examining early postwar trucks, one must realize that most of what existed was what was there before the war. Those vehicles would be replaced slowly as new trucks became available. Truck manufacturers actually began to build a limited number of vehicles for civilian use as early as mid-1944, but the government's War Production Board had the complete say as to whom they would be sold. Critical military supply operations, of course, held top priority. Once the war ended, manufacturers were deluged with floods of orders, creating a backlog of deliveries that lasted up to three years. Most manufacturers didn't even give any thought to introducing any new or improved models at this time, so that available new trucks were basically the same models that were available just before the war in 1940–1941. New trucks were essentially rationed out in small lots to the larger companies while a smalltime operator might have to wait a year or two for delivery on a single unit.

There was a definite swing to tractor-semi trailers in most parts of the country, especially in over-the-road service. In 1940, Mack had finally replaced its antique-looking B types (BM-BX-BQ) with the new L models (LF to LJ). This kept truck styling, somewhat, in sight of automotive styling as other manufacturers made similar advancements as well. Diesel-powered trucks had begun to appear in the mid-1930s, enjoying some popularity, especially on the West Coast and in heavy-duty applications nationwide. Although several makes of engines, such as Buda, Hercules, and Waukesha, were available, it was Cummins that rose to the top as the most dependable of the stock diesel engines.

In 1938, Mack introduced its own diesel engine, the sickly ED-519, most of which fell rapidly to repowering with a Cummins or Buda diesel. The 519 was bored-out to a 605 by 1940, but it didn't help much. General Motors purchased Gray Marine in 1939, which gave them their famous 4-71 and 6-71 two-cycle diesels, known so well for their high-pitched song and acrid-smelling exhaust.

Popular Trucks of the Day

Some of the more popular trucks seen on the road in this period were Autocar's Tough C-70 and C-90 gas jobs, and their cab-over-engine companion models, the U-70 and U-90. Also, their Cummins diesel-powered DC-100 series was always popular, particularly with the drivers, and ranks as an all-time big-truck classic.

Other commonly favored gas jobs were International's K8-8s, 10s, and 11s; White's WC-22 Mustangs, and the Big 28s; and GMC's 700 and 900 series. Other heavy hitters in the big-truck field were Mack LFs and LJs. The LJ had a 707-ci gas engine so brawny that a good one could give even a 200-horsepower Cummins diesel a run for its money.

Another hot truck was a 260 Brockway. Powered with a 572-ci Continental gas engine, it was also capable of really "waling the dog," and a well-tuned one usually had a nice sharp rattle to the exhaust.

In the early postwar era, Federal and Ward LaFrance, both of which produced many highway-type tractors, enjoyed some popularity. Often the Ward LaFrances were equipped with 150- or 200-horsepower Cummins diesels and were quite impressive, in a rather brutish way. But, by the 1950s, they were specializing almost exclusively in fire equipment, while Federal limited its production mostly to highway department–type vehicles, and export models.

Dodges and Fords were numerous as highway trucks and tractors, although most were intended for light- or medium-duty jobs such as pulling moving vans or car carriers. It was not uncommon, though, to see one salted down with a real load and working hard to haul it.

Sterlings were quite popular too; best remembered as The Horse for tremendous over-sized loads on low-boys, many were employed as trucks and tractors in highway service out West. In the East many found favor as dumpers, mixers, or as tractors for sand and gravel outfits. Power was supplied by big-cube Waukesha gas engines and Cummins diesels.

The big Kenworths and Peterbilts used out West were mostly long-chassised trucks or tractors with super-charged diesel engines for operations in the mountains. Always very attractive in both conventional and cab-over-engine (COE) form, it was quite a thrill to see one sneak in to the East Coast with its long, West Coast, refrigerated trailer, loaded with swinging beef.

Such was the array of trucks working the highway roads in our country in the immediate postwar era. The straight jobs and single-axle tractor-trailers dominated in the East, and the four- and five-axle combination units ruled the West. A few ex-military vehicles had been pressed into service but they, for the most part, were not really practical in civilian service. So, most of the truckers had to wait for things to get better. Eventually they did.

Big Trucks Take Over

Slowly, as the nation's highways began to improve, so did the trucks that ran them. As the trucks improved, so did the service, and as a result, so did business. State size and weight restrictions began to increase, despite the plaintive cries of the railroad lobbyist's efforts to prevent it. By the early 1950s, most states had begun to recognize the tandem-axle trailer, and length limits had increased from the prewar 40 feet to 45 feet. Appropriately, weight limits on three-axle units had risen from 45,000 to 50,000 pounds, while the new tandems were allowed 60,000 pounds in most states. In western states where five-axle tractor-trailers and six-axle truck and full-trailer combinations were operated, the maximum was usually closer to 70,000 pounds.

Truck operators who were able to field equipment that was capable of carrying maximum loads while maintaining acceptable road speeds in this era were few and far between. Often, companies and even owner-operators made do with older or underpowered trucks as a matter of financial necessity. Some were just plain cheap, like using a boy to do a man's job.

Conversely, it was not unusual to see a big, brawny Brockway, or even an Autocar diesel, in service where small trailers or light loads were an everyday occurrence. Basically, trucking companies used what was available.

Freight companies in the Northeast tended to stick more with company-owned equipment, and therefore the trucks they ran tended to be less than exciting. Inevitably, many of their drivers would not be denied in expressing their own fascinations, and their regular tractors might be trimmed extravagantly with self-bought chrome trim, windshield visors, marker lights, or spot lights. It was commonly known in the underground that some drivers even had a little unauthorized tuning done on the engine in search of a few extra horses or rpms. The yen for individuality was difficult to satisfy, especially when one's reputation at the office stop gabble was at stake.

In the Midwest, the long-haul carriers often preferred to hire owner-operators, guys who owned their own tractors and leased out to larger freight companies. Some operated a core of company-owned trucks, some just local pickup and delivery units, and some a portion of their road equipment. The benefits of this system were that the company had more control over expanding or shrinking the fleet to meet varying business needs.

For the owner-operator, freedom was the major incentive: freedom to operate the type of equipment he desired, and to trim it, tune it, and drive it the way he wanted. But with these freedoms came tremendous responsibilities, as he needed to be very proficient, not only as a driver, but as a mechanic, bookkeeper, salesman, lawyer, horse trader, and general businessman. Many owner-operators pulled steadily for one company year after year, whereas others moved about regularly, often following seasonal business patterns. This is why we would often see a tractor pulling a load it didn't seem very well suited for.

But these were the guys that many of us envied. We watched as they rolled in from the West: Daniels, TransAmerican, Chicago Express, Midwest Emery, Safeway Middle Atlantic. Swinging beef, produce, steel, and general freight were pulled by big Autocars, Macks, Diamond Ts, and Hendricksons; you name it, they had it. Trucks had license tags across the bumpers, bug screens, West Coast mirrors, twin spotlights, huge air-horns. Most of the big stuff out of the West was diesel powered. There were a few Mack diesels, and some screamin' jimmies, and maybe a few smoky Buda engines, but the force to deal with was the guys with the Cummins power. Just try to pass that guy with the big Diamond T with a two-hundred Cummins in there, and he'll just pull the Brownie back a notch and shatter your ear drums through a Gutter Donaldson muffler. "My one-seventy-five throws enough fire-pulling Tuscarora Mountain to read the newspaper by," or "that old A-Car had forty-eight grand on the other night, but she had enough left to push a load of steel over Ceasson Mountain." So the stories went. What an era!

—Dave Read

Autocar Company

Competition was fierce among the numerous truck manufacturers in the early 1900s. Those that survived did so in part because they were better trucks, built and sold by companies that knew how to please the customers who purchased the product. Such was the case with the Autocar Company, which traces its beginnings to the founding of the Pittsburgh Motor Car Company of Pittsburgh, Pennsylvania, by brothers Louis S. and John S. Clark in 1897. They started by building motorized tricycles and a car called the Pittsburger. Soon after, the company name was changed to the Autocar Company, and at the turn of the century the company moved to Ardmore, Pennsylvania.

In 1907, they started to experiment with commercial vehicles. Their success with commercial vehicles was so great that by 1911 they had discontinued the passenger cars. Their first truck models were Type XVIII and Type XXI. According to the book Motor Trucks of America Vol. 5, published by the B.F. Goodrich Company, in 1917 the chassis price for the model 21F was $1,650. These were discontinued in 1926 after a total production of more than 30,000, many of which were buses used in World War I by the United States, Canada, and Great Britain. The first engine was an 18.1-horsepower, two-cylinder job, followed by a four-cylinder underseat engine.

A new series of conventional trucks was introduced in 1926, from 1- to 7-ton capacities. By the early 1930s, Autocar had started making cabs and chassis for off-highway construction. The early Autocars were the cab-over-engine type. Then in 1933, the cab-over was reintroduced as the U series, which carried on into the 1950s. Autocar used their own engines, but by 1935, they were also using Waukesha and Cummins diesels in their DC series, which carried up into the 1960s. Production began on a large scale in 1940 when Autocar began making vehicles for World War II military use. After the war, civilian production began and in 1946, a total of 5,320 trucks were produced.

Autocar introduced the all-new driver cab in the early 1950s, discontinuing the flat windshield style. However, the flat windshield cab was still used in the integral sleeper version until 1952. In 1955, Autocar introduced a new A series that sported an aluminum chassis. The C line also existed in the 1950s. With financial problems on the horizon, Autocar was acquired by the White Motor Company in 1953, and production was moved to Exton, Pennsylvania. The Autocar became the top of the line for White, primarily used in logging, mining, quarrying, and the oil industry. Aluminum construction reduced the weight of the truck considerably and increased the payload by 2 tons. Given the wide variety of existing models in the 1950s, Autocars were built more on a custom basis, offering a wide range of gearboxes and axles, as well as engines, such as Cummins, Caterpillar, Detroit Hall-Scott, and the White gasoline engine. Diesel engine horsepower ranged anywhere from 220 up to 600, with gearboxes up to 13 speeds.

The models continued to be offered into the 1960s, through the 1970s, and the 1980s even saw the introduction of a few new models. In 1980, production at the Exton plant was discontinued and moved to Ogden, Utah. Unfortunately, the Autocar name was dropped in July 1995.

The U model also came in a tractor version. This one was used for hauling more than 22,000 bottles of soda for the Coca-Cola Company on the Trailmobile trailer.
A.T.H.S. Zoe James Library

Autocar trucks were used in every segment of trucking. Here we have a DCU 75T on a 147-inch wheelbase. An HRFB 180 engine supplies the power and is matched up to a Fuller R96 transmission, the whole rig riding on 10:00/22 tires. H. B. Sparrow & Sons of Scranton, South Carolina, was the owner of this Autocar and Dorsey produce trailer. *Autocar Trucks*

Michigan haulers had some of their own breeds of trucks. This eight-axle dump truck and trailer worked for Hamlin-McCain Inc. of South Lyon, Michigan. A double bumper and construction-type fenders give this Autocar the tough look. *Neil Sherff*

Here we have a sleeper cab on a tandem-axle tractor. OK Tire Stores owned the DC75 tractor and Brown trailer. The picture was taken in California. *Brian Williams*

One of the smaller models in the DC series was this DC-65-T. It sports the new driver cab and rides on 11:00/22 tires. Wagmans Transfer Corp. of Medford, Massachusetts, was the proud owner. *Autocar Trucks*

The DC100 series was designed for the Western trucker. This 1951 model has the new driver cab running on 11:00/22 tires on a 170-inch wheelbase, pulling two 20-foot Trailmobile flatbed trailers for Capital Freight Lines of Sacramento, California, as a contract carrier. *Autocar Trucks*

The DC100s were a popular truck, especially among the Western truckers. This rugged-looking Autocar was set up as a straight truck, but was rarely seen with a sleeper cab. A coating of snow blankets the truck. *Ron Adams Collection*

The big DC100 series was popular in the West. Here we see a DC10062 riding on 10:00/20 tires with a Page & Page tag-along third axle. Dave Martin of El Cajon, California, owned this truck-trailer combination for hauling cement blocks and building materials. *Autocar Trucks*

Here we have another DC10062 as a truck tractor with the same components as the previous photo. The wheelbases ranged anywhere from 210 to 252 inches. Again, Dave Martin of El Cajon, California, was the owner. *Autocar Trucks*

The DC100 was available in several versions—the owner of this tractor chose the integral sleeper. Sleeper cabs were very popular with long-distance refrigerated haulers. Zero Refrigerated Lines Inc. of San Antonio, Texas, leased this tractor and Lufkin trailer. *Ron Adams Collection*

Another truck-trailer combination was this C-10062-N. The rig runs on 10:00/22 tires, has a Page & Page third-axle attachment, and is powered by a 1091 B Hall-Scott butane gas engine. Notice the special butane tanks that were installed by the customer, Rockgas Service Company of El Cajon, California. *Autocar Trucks*

Here is another DC100 with a set of Western double trailers. The Sunland Olive Company was the owner of this outfit. Because single-axle conventional tractors were not too common in the West, this was a rare unit.
Brian Williams

Still in the DC series but slightly different was this DC10264. It ran on 10:00/20 tires and was powered by a 220-horsepower JP diesel engine with a 4x3 transmission. Hunsaker Trucking contractors of Carrolton, Texas, hauled this 255,000-pound transformer on a Lufkin low-boy trailer. The overall length stretched out to 87 feet.
Autocar Trucks

The A100 series captured the Western truckers, as did the DC100 series. Walter Strauss and Son of Fort Worth, Texas, used several of these A100s for hauling frozen products and produce out of Texas in the Lufkin trailer.
Neil Sherff

15

Autocars were tough trucks in the logging business. The Douglas Veneer Company of Roseburg, Oregon, put this A10464 to work with a 250-horsepower diesel engine and a 4x4 transmission. The wheelbase on this tractor was 246 inches. *Autocar Trucks*

This AW10264 had a 196-inch wheelbase. The power came from a 335-horsepower Cummins diesel engine with a 12-speed main transmission riding on 11:00/20 tires. Eveready Freight Service of Buena Vista, Colorado, put this rig to work. *Autocar Trucks*

Produce hauling was usually long-distance trips. Tractors were usually sleeper equipped, whether it was a cab-over-engine or a conventional type such as this Autocar DC75 with a Great Dane reefer trailer. Fender mirrors, dual air horns and stacks, and an air conditioner for summer comfort were among the extras that fancied up this tractor. The picture was taken at the produce center in Philadelphia, Pennsylvania. *Robert J. Parrish*

Autocars were very popular in the dump truck segment. Ray Trucking Company of Dedham, Massachusetts, owned the DC9964. A 190-horsepower diesel engine, a 15-speed transmission, a 16,000-pound-capacity front axle, and a 50,000-pound rear axle were placed between a 171-inch wheelbase and rode on 11:00/24 tires. *Autocar Trucks*

Another dump truck from Autocar was this DC20364 used for the coal mines. The power source is a 300-horsepower diesel engine hooked up to a four-speed main and three-speed auxiliary transmission with a 25,000-pound front axle and 70,000-pound rear axle. All the components are on a 220-inch wheelbase riding on 14:00/24 tires for Amherst Coal Company in Charleston, West Virginia. *Autocar Trucks*

The construction industry got a big lift from this Model AP-15 dump truck. This 4x2, 15-ton-capacity off-highway rear dumper had the Autocar driver cab, FE 18 front axle with a 10B1120 transmission, and a NH-220 Cummins diesel engine. The AP-15 was the smallest in a series of four. *Autocar Trucks*

The Shell Oil Company used this C-65-T to deliver gasoline to their chain of service stations. The C-65-T had a 142-inch wheelbase, a V-8 gasoline engine, and rode on 11:00/20-inch tires. The trailer was a Butler with a capacity of 6,490 gallons. *Autocar Trucks*

This C-85-T had a 142-inch wheelbase, the new driver cab, a V-8 engine, and ran on 11:00/22 tires. H. M. Gould Trucking Company of East Walpole, Massachusetts, was the owner of this tractor and Fruehauf flatbed trailer. They were a contract hauler for Bird and Son of East Walpole to haul rolls of paper. *Autocar Trucks*

Autocar also made a cab-over-engine known as the U model. This U-50 is on a 142-inch wheelbase with a 20-foot body that was built by Yankee Motor Bodies Corporation for hauling lumber. Rollers and a hydraulic tailgate make unloading real easy for the Penberthy Lumber Company in Los Angeles, California. *Autocar Trucks*

CHAPTER 2

Brockway Motor Truck Company

Although the first Brockway truck was made in 1912, the company's roots go back to 1851 when William Brockway started his carriage business in Homer, New York. William's son George Brockway started the Brockway Motor Truck Company in Cortland, New York, with $100,000. The first Brockway was a high wheeler similar to the appearance of the 1912 Chase truck. In 1913–1914, they sold for $1,450 to $1,925 depending on the model. Brockway built 587 Class B Liberty trucks for the military during World War I.

Civilian truck production started again in 1919. In 1920, the models started with a 1-ton that sold for $2,100 and went up to a 5-ton that sold for $5,000, using a design that stayed basically the same through the early 1920s. Early Brockways used Continental engines, and in 1925 they started using the Wisconsin engine. The wheelbases ranged from 153 inches on the 1-ton model up to 174 inches on the 5-ton model. Brockway expanded in 1928 with the purchase of the Indiana Truck Corporation with combined assets of $9 million. Also in that year, production totaled over 5,500 units with net profits of over $1 million. The purchase of Indiana opened the westward market and into some foreign countries. However, Indiana ownership lasted only four years because of the depression. Brockway was forced to sell and the White Motor Company became the new owners of the Indiana Truck Corporation.

In 1934, Brockway introduced the Model V1200, one of the largest trucks in the United States at that time. Powered by a 240-horsepower V-12 American LaFrance engine, top speed was 45 miles per hour and the chassis cost was $10,500. Since a number of states had weight limits per axle, sales of the V1200 were limited and the model was available only through 1937. The model line ranged up to 15 tons, including a third axle version for the heaviest trucks. As World War II began, Brockway, like many other manufacturers, was again under contract with the military. Brockway built 1,237 trucks for civilian use in 1944. Shortly after the war, they introduced the new 260 series. A sleeper cab truck tractor was available at this time. In 1946, Brockway built 4,212 trucks, but then in 1948 production dropped to 2,919 units. Up to this point, Brockway was still using the Continental gas engine. The models ranged from the 88 series to the 260 series. Sales continued to slip, and by 1952 total sales were 1,752 units, dropping further to 611 units by 1954, representing only 1 percent of the market.

Brockway was infused with new life when Mack Trucks purchased the company in 1956. In 1957, Brockway introduced off-highway oil field rigs and heavy-duty short tractors, and in 1958, the new Huskie series. The Model 258 measured 87 inches from bumper to back of cab. In 1960 they offered a new sleeper cab. In 1962 the Huskie emblem turned from chrome to gold to celebrate Brockway's 50th anniversary. Around this time Continental and Cummins diesel engines were offered, and Brockway made its first cab-over-engine model—a modified F series Mack cab. They became very popular and at this time Detroit Diesel engines were added to the engine line. The Caterpillar diesel engine also became available in 1965.

The Husketeer series, which was the low-profile cab-over-engine, was introduced in 1970. In 1975, Brockway filled an order for Tran to make 575 trucks. In 1977, they made trucks with engines up to 500 horsepower that were capable of hauling up to 53,000 pounds. But at this time, the company was in trouble. Because of financial problems and difficulties with the new anti-skid brake legislation, Mack decided to shut down Brockway permanently.

Many of the manufacturers started new models in the late 1940s that carried over into the 1950s for several years. The Model 260 was a very popular model for Brockway. Southern Brokerage Company of Miami, Florida, had this sleeper model running north to the Midwestern states. It is probably powered by a Cummins diesel. *Joe Wanchura*

Louis Barber of Leesburg, New Jersey, did a splendid restoration job on his 1951 Model 260-X Brockway. It was around this time the Brockway started using the three-piece curved windshield. The flat windshield was also being used well into the 1950s. *Don MacKenzie*

Brockways were not only used by trucking companies, but also by private carriers. Shell Oil Company used their Model 260 to pull a gasoline trailer. Louvers on the sides of the hood were common on a lot of trucks. *Shell Oil Co.*

This early-1950s Model 154 Brockway ran out of Florida and was probably waiting for a load for the long journey back home. *Ron Adams Collection*

The smiling gentleman standing beside this Model 154 Brockway sleeper and Fruehauf trailer was the proud owner or driver of this rig for Cash & Carry Produce Company of Chattanooga, Tennessee. The source of power in this rig was probably a Continental gas engine, which Brockway used for many years. *Ron Adams Collection*

A coating of snow from Mother Nature blanketed the ground while this Model 260 Brockway took a break. Daniels Motor Freight of Warren, Ohio, had a number of open-top trailers, which were used for overhead loading. *Neil Sherff*

Another famous Brockway was this Model 154. The standard engine was a Continental 572-ci with a standard wheelbase of 144 inches. Chemical Tank Lines of Downingtown, Pennsylvania, had a fleet of Brockways, such as this one at a refinery to pick up a load of fuel. *Chemical-Leaman Inc.*

The 255 was another Brockway model. Although the standard engine was a Continental, this one was powered by a Cummins diesel. The change from gas to diesel must have been made after 1962 because that was the first year that Brockway started using the Cummins.
Joe Wanchura

This 255 was used to deliver gasoline for Humble Oil and Refining Company in Pelham Manor, New York. Dave Reed drove this truck early in his 40-year driving career.
Dave Reed

This circa-1958 Model 257 is shown in a sleeper cab version. The script on the side of the hood reveals that it was powered by a Cummins diesel, either a 180- or a 195-horsepower engine. Notice that the small round mirrors were still being used at this time. *Brockway*

In 1958, Brockway started the new Huskie series. One of the models was the 158 cargo, which was a straight truck. L. A. Milan chose one to do hauling for Howe and French, who were manufacturers of chemicals and solvents. Both diesel and gas were offered as the source of power. *Brockway*

Marr Scaffolding Company of South Boston, Massachusetts, was another customer that used the 158 cargo model. Photographed on the job site, the scaffolding is visible in the background. *Brockway*

Another model in the Huskie series was the 260. Cummins diesel engines were standard with 180, 195, or 220 horsepower. This 260 was powered by a 220-horsepower diesel engine. Michigan Screw Products in Centerline, Michigan, had their Model 260 hooked to a Fruehauf spread-axle trailer. *Neil Sherff*

The 260 fit in almost every part of trucking. The application here is being hooked to a Heil gasoline tank trailer. Marcey's Oil Company of Provincetown, Massachusetts, decided to fancy up their 260 with plenty of extra chrome and did a good job of it. *Brockway*

Chemical-Leaman Tank Lines of Downingtown, Pennsylvania, had a large fleet of trucks in the liquid bulk hauling business. They also had owner-operator leased tractors such as this Model 258. The driver had the option to select a sleeper cab for resting while on the road. *Neil Sherff*

By the end of the 1950s, double 40-foot trailers were starting to come into use. Many carriers, including Penn Yan Express of Penn Yan, New York, used them on the Massachusetts, Ohio, and Indiana turnpikes and on the New York State Thruway. On this run, Penn Yan decided to hook up a Model 258 Brockway to pull two Strick 40-foot trailers. *Ron Adams Collection*

Chevrolet

In 1912, William Crapo Durant started building cars designed by Louis Chevrolet; despite the cars carrying his name, Chevrolet left the company in 1913. But the Chevrolet line was a success and was running right along with the rest of the well-known brands of this time. In 1918, Chevrolet started building trucks with a half-ton and a 1-ton model. They were not unusual, with solid rubber tires and a 225-ci four-cylinder overhead-valve engine. The first year, truck production totaled 879. By the time 1919 came to an end, production totaled 7,300 trucks.

In 1925, the company offered a six-wheel trailering-axle version in the H series. By 1929 total Chevrolet truck production had reached one-half million. For the year 1930 alone, Chevrolet sold more than 188,000 trucks. In 1930, the Martin-Parry Body Company was acquired and their bodies were fitted on the Chevrolet trucks along with bodies from other brand commercial manufacturers.

By the early 1930s, the Chevrolet commercial engine developed 46 horsepower. After a redesign and improvements made in 1933, Chevrolet outpaced Ford in truck production for the first time and would soon have 10 manufacturing plants nationwide. In 1936, truck tractors were produced and sold well. They produced their first cab-over-engine in 1937 but for export only, with an optional 77-horsepower diesel engine. The rest of the Chevrolet truck line used a 216-ci six-cylinder engine that put out 78 horsepower. During this time, Chevrolet was working on the development of an automatic transmission.

As World War II started, Chevrolet played its part in war production, building a total of over 131,000 trucks in 1943–1944. In the postwar years 1946 and 1947, Chevrolet used the 1942 designs, with new designs starting in 1948.

In 1952, a 90-horsepower Detroit Diesel engine was a rarely used option. Restyling of the conventional truck came in 1954 with a new one-piece windshield. In 1955, Chevrolet offered a four-speed Hydra-matic transmission in all models and sold a record 393,315 commercial trucks that year, making them the largest truck maker in the United States with 31 percent of the market. Tubeless tires became standard in 1956 and V-8 engines were available in most trucks. A new line of cab-over-engine models came in 1960, with gross combination weight (GCW) up to 40,000 pounds. The four-cylinder Detroit Diesel was an option, but larger diesel engines were available for the heavy-duty trucks.

In 1962, the 8 millionth Chevrolet truck was sold. Through the 1960s Chevrolet truck design remained the same. In 1969, Chevrolet entered the heavy truck market with their new Titan 90, which had a GCW of 65,000 pounds. This cab was similar to the GMC Astro, which was also introduced shortly before. The tilt-cab was available as a 4x2 and 6x4 version. Engine options included Detroit Diesel's V-6, V-8, and V-12 engines with up to 390 horsepower, and Cummins diesels up to 319 horsepower. In 1977, Chevrolet introduced the Bison, which was equal to the GMC General. This new 6x4 was rated for 80,000-pound gross combination weight. The diesel engines were either from Cummins or Detroit Diesel with up to 490 horsepower with a standard five-speed automatic transmission. Chevrolet has come a long way and has kept up with the competition, which suggests they will be around a while longer.

This design started in 1948 but continued into 1953. The Pacific Grocery Company in Everett, Washington, decided to purchase a Brown truck body and place it on this Chevrolet straight truck. Pacific Grocery was a distributor for Olympia Beer. *Ron Adams Collection*

Standard Generator Service Company in St. Louis, Missouri, had this Supercargo trailer painted with an eye-catching design and then decided to make this Chevrolet tractor the power partner to the trailer. Tractor and trailer make a rather handsome pair. *Andrews Industries*

The cab-over-engine design was also started in 1948 and continued into 1953, the same as the conventional. Complete Auto Transit Company in St. Louis, Missouri, used this Chevrolet cab-over-engine tractor to haul new cars. This load is early-1950s Chevrolet cars and one pickup. *Ron Adams Collection*

Another early-1950s Chevrolet cab-over-engine tractor was serving its time for Riss & Co. of Denver, Colorado, pulling a Fruehauf open-top trailer. At this time, Riss & Co. covered the southwest states, but in the later years, went to the East Coast and New England. *Ron Adams Collection*

This circa-1952 Chevrolet is a restoration job that was at the American Truck Historical Society annual convention in Schaumburg, Illinois, in 1987. The trailer looks like it could be a homemade one. Harold Edwards of Omaha, Illinois, was the owner at this time. *Ron Adams*

Sites Freightlines of Portland, Oregon, purchased a fleet of Chevrolet trucks for their city delivery work. Notice that the grille style has changed in 1954. The fenders, hood, and cab remained basically the same as the early-1950s model. *Sites Freightlines*

For 1955–1956, the cab design changed again. This 5700 series was equipped with a sleeper cab. Judging from the frame length, it looks like this could be a chassis with a body as a straight truck instead of a truck tractor. *Ron Adams Collection*

These tractors were used for over the road, but they were also used as city delivery tractors with many of the big trucking companies. Lee Way Motor Freight of Oklahoma City, Oklahoma, had this one doing city pickup and delivery work along with this Fruehauf city delivery trailer. Notice the antenna for the two-way system that many city fleets had. *Lee Way Motor Freight*

Another Chevrolet tractor of the same style was this 5100 series, powered by a V-8 engine. A Fruehauf Aero-Van trailer of the late 1940s was teamed up with this tractor for Var's Express and Transfer Company, location unknown. *Ron Adams Collection*

In 1958, the new Viking series went into production. The chassis was the Viking 60 series, and the cab and body were made by the Swab Wagon Company. The 22-foot unit was making deliveries for Holsum Bread. *Swab Wagon Co.*

Although this new style cab-over-engine did not come out until 1960, the engineering and designing was done in the late 1950s. Eugene Cook of Plant City, Florida, decided to buy himself one of these new tilt-cab trucks. Produce was the commodity he hauled from Florida to the market in the Northeast. *Harry Patterson*

Although they were not the most powerful trucks on the road, they got the job done just the same. North American Van Lines of Fort Wayne, Indiana, had this Chevrolet leased to them with an aftermarket sleeper added to it. Moving household goods was the job for this rig. *Harry Patterson*

Engel Bros. Moving Company of Elizabeth, New Jersey, was another carrier of household goods. Chevrolet tractors such as this one seemed to be popular in this kind of business at this time. Notice all the license plates that trucks had to display when traveling across country. *Harry Patterson*

Diamond T

C. A. Tilt started manufacturing passenger cars in 1907. In 1911, although there were numerous makes of trucks already on the market, one of Tilt's customers came to him and said he wanted a truck. Tilt complied, building a chain drive model with a 40-horsepower Continental and a three-speed transmission. He named the truck Diamond T, and legend has it that it was still in service in the Chicago area some 20 years later.

Tilt continued building trucks. In 1912, the largest model was a 5-ton job that sold for $3,350. During the early 1910s, a number of different models were made in different price ranges. In 1916, the facilities in north Chicago became inadequate and a new factory was built in southwest Chicago. A new 1,000-foot assembly line aided the production of 1,500 3-ton Liberty trucks during the 18 months of World War I. After this accomplishment, the military ordered an additional 2,000 units.

After the war, the company focused on expanding their dealerships. Through the 1920s, they offered a variety of models in weight classes from 1-tons up to six-wheel 12-ton models. In 1933, a whole new style of cab was introduced, and in 1936 a new light diesel line came into existence.

Over time, Diamond T developed a reputation for making big trucks, but they also made pickup trucks and panel trucks. For long hauls, sleeper cabs were also available. Like every other manufacturer, Diamond T turned to making military vehicles during World War II, manufacturing more than 50,000 units of varying

models. After the war, civilian production started again. The postwar design was the same as the prewar design, and the Diamond T line consisted of 14 models. In 1946, C.A. Tilt retired from the company. Production reached 10,475 units in 1947 and a record 10,651 units in 1948.

In 1951, lighter models were dropped and they focused mainly on the larger models from the 660 to the big 951. The larger trucks were powered by Cummins and Buda diesel engines up to 300 horsepower. Diamond T also started using certain International cabs and Hall-Scott engines. In 1958, the White Motor Company, which had bought out REO Motor Truck Company the year before, purchased Diamond T; they moved operations to the REO plant in Lansing, Michigan, two years later. By the mid-1960s, Caterpillar and Detroit Diesel engines were offered in the six-wheeled models. In 1967, both REO and Diamond T were merged by White and became known as Diamond REO. Although Diamond REO trucks are still made today, the White Company has no part in the ownership.

Sometimes the make of certain cabs can fool you. Though this looked like an International cab, it was an International as used by Diamond T. Hendrickson also used this cab on some of their trucks. Mother's Cookies, location unknown, used this Diamond T tractor and unknown–brand name trailer to transport their products. *Ron Adams Collection, Bev. Washburn Studios*

This grille and cab style was the new style of the 1950s for Diamond T. This Model 723 with the integral sleeper cab and Dorsey trailer was owned by L. A. Keegstra Produce of Grand Rapids, Michigan. *Dorsey Trailers*

Diamond T trucks seemed to be very popular with the Michigan steel haulers. Truck-trailer combinations such as this were a common site on the highways of Michigan, Indiana, and Ohio. Hess Cartage Company of Melvindale, Michigan, was one of the companies who used this kind of setup. *Neil Sherff*

Before the days of his big 951 Diamond T, B. C. Fry of Independence, Iowa, did his trucking in this circa-1954–1955 Diamond T and Dorsey reefer trailer. Many chrome extras were added by Fry to fancy up his rig. Fry became a legend of the highway with his big, powerful 1959 951 Diamond T. *Bob Ward*

Some models offered two styles of radiators, a flat front and the grille style. This 723 model shows the chrome bar–style grille. The owner of the tractor was probably Conklin Truck Lines, which was part of the Keeshin Freight System. The Fruehauf Aero-Van trailer belonged to Hail Freight Lines. *Neil Sherff*

The other style radiator is this flat-front aluminum radiator shell. Another Diamond T Model 723, in 1953, was owned by Midwest Freight Forwarding Company of Chicago, Illinois. All three trailers were Fruehaufs. *Ron Adams Collection*

The Model 921 was available in three versions. The 921D had six chrome bars and axle forward, the 921DB had the axle back, and the 921DF had the axle forward with the aluminum flat-front radiator as shown in this photo. Christopher Oil Company of Tucson, Arizona, owned this truck-trailer tanker combination. *Ron Adams Collection*

Another 921DF, this time as a log hauler. The wheelbases ranged anywhere from 170 to 242 inches. Harry S. Note of Medford, Oregon, owned this log-hauling rig. Notice the old-style turn signal. *Ron Adams Collection*

Another Diamond T series was the 931. This 931F was owned by Little Audrey's Transportation Company of Fremont, Nebraska. The trailer is a Strick reefer. The wheelbases on this model ranged from 163 to 247 inches. The standard engine was a Cummins NH-220, but the options were from 262 to 335 horsepower. *Ron Adams Collection*

The Model 921C was Diamond T's cab-over-engine tractor. The engines were Cummins diesels with up to 262 horsepower on a wheelbase up to 190 inches. This 921C was leased to Midwest Emery Freight System of Chicago, Illinois, pulling a Highway reefer trailer. *Neil Sherff*

The 921C was also available in a single-axle version. This was also Cummins powered with anywhere from 190 to 300 horsepower. The wheelbases ranged from 114 to 135 inches. The Orange Thorpe Hay Company of Artesia, California, used their 921C to pull two Utility flatbed trailers to haul hay. *Utility Trailer Co.*

The Model 951 was the biggest one of them all from Diamond T. The earlier 951s were powered by Buda diesels but later they were powered also by Cummins or Detroit Diesel. The wheelbases ranged from 170 to 242 inches. This particular 951 Diamond T is powered by a V-12 Detroit Diesel engine with 475 horsepower pulling a Dorsey reefer trailer. B. C. Fry of Independence, Iowa, was the owner and it was leased to several carriers like Curtis of Denver, Colorado; Caravelle Express of Norfolk, Nebraska; and Safeway Truck Lines of Chicago, Illinois. *Neil Sherff*

CHAPTER 5

Dodge Trucks

Parrish & Clark in Tulsa, Oklahoma, had been a new car dealer since 1916 and with Dodge since 1941. This 1948 2-ton Dodge with the oil field bed was made in 1948. The two men on the far right are Dick and Ralph Fahrenwald. Dick was the truck manager and Ralph was general sales manager. The two men on the left are unknown. *Ron Adams Collection*

Starting with a small machine shop in Detroit, John and Horace Dodge supplied 3,000 transmissions to Ransom Eli Olds by 1902 and later supplied axles, engines, and transmissions to Henry Ford. They made a fortune doing this, but they decided it was time to venture into manufacturing their own cars. By the end of 1914, 249 Dodge Brothers cars rolled out of the factory in Detroit. The following year, 45,000 vehicles left the factory, making Dodge third in the industry. In 1916, they started fitting light truck bodies on the Dodge chassis. They were built as ambulances for the war in Europe. The civilian version was a screenside. By the end of 1918, the U.S. military bought 2,644 screenside trucks.

Around this same time, a tractor-trailer unit was built. By 1920, Dodge became the number two producer. Brothers John and Horace both died the same year. After 18,000 of the 22,000-employee workforce was laid off in 1921 due to a recession, Dodge fell into third place. Dodge's affiliation with Graham became the Dodge truck division in 1924. The 1-ton Model A sold for $2,495. The Dodge factory was expanded in 1922 and produced 600 vehicles per day. By 1923, Dodge fell into sixth place. At this time the Dodge widows decided to sell the company and in 1925 received a cash purchase of $146 million. In 1925 Dodge bought controlling interest in Graham Brothers' trucks. In 1927, Dodge Brothers was sold

to Chrysler for a $170 million stock transaction. As Chrysler took over, Graham trucks were immediately phased out.

By 1930, Dodge was fourth in truck manufacturing, with a total of 15,558 delivered that year. In 1936, the 3-ton K63V truck tractors were used to pull fleet trailers coast to coast for U.S. Truck Company. Production neared 65,000 in 1937 with a listing of 14 models. A new $6 million plant was built in Warren, Michigan, which made 98 percent of all Dodge trucks. The entire model line was redesigned in 1939 to celebrate Dodge's 25th anniversary. The same year Dodge also offered a standard diesel engine, including the 3-ton truck tractors. The first cab-over-engine design came in 1940 with the Series VLA in sleeper cab form, with an optional 95-horsepower diesel engine.

In 1942, production was changed over to defense work. Over 539,000 military trucks were totally redesigned in 1948, and a new plant was built in San Leandro, California. A one-piece curved windshield was introduced in 1954 on the lighter trucks. Also, new engines were offered along with many other options. A whole new line of Dodge trucks was introduced for 1951. The new line brought styling changes and a broader selection of models. The 2 1/2-ton J series cab-over had the shortest turning radius of any cab-over truck that year. By 1955, V-8 engines were made available for the entire truck line. The Power-Dome V-8 hemi engine put out 145 horsepower. In 1957 a new range of tandem-axle trucks were produced and powered by engines with 201 or 232 horsepower. In 1959, the three heaviest models were the D-800 and D-900, and the T-900, which was the three-axle model.

In 1960, swing-out fenders were introduced for easier engine access, along with the new C model which featured 6x4 trucks with a gross combined weight rating up to 53,000 pounds. Turbocharged Cummins diesel engines were available. The largest Dodge came in 1962—the three-axle Series 1000 rated at 5-ton. The Cummins NH-220 diesel was the power source. The 900 and 1000 series were built in standard or COE tilt-cab version. They were powered by gasoline or diesel including V-6 or V-8 Cummins. The LN1000 and LNT 1000 were introduced in 1964 with production lasting through 1975. Heavy cement mixer chassis were also built by Dodge and by 1965 an 8x4 with trailing-axle truck tractor was built for an 80-ton gross combined weight, as was a 10x4 cement mixer.

By 1970, Dodge entered the long-distance hauling service with the LM100 COE tilt-cab. The engine options were a 318-horsepower Detroit Diesel V-8 and the 335-horsepower turbocharged Cummins diesel V-8. The year 1971 saw the introduction of the Big Horn D-9500, available as a three-axle diesel-powered truck tractor. By the end of 1975, Dodge discontinued all its heavy-duty trucks because of new government regulations and poor profits. A total of only 261 Big Horns were built through their three-year production.

This cab style was introduced in 1948. This 1949 3-ton Model B-1 was owned by Central States Steel of Davenport, Iowa. The unknown driver is securing the tarp for cargo protection on this Fruehauf half-top trailer. *Dick Copello*

Mid-Continent Airlines maintained a fleet of aviation gasoline fueling trucks. In this nine-truck fleet, the first was a B-1 series Dodge, which was the of 1949 era. *Columbian Steel Tank Co.*

Another Dodge of the B-3 series was this tandem-axle dump truck. After years of use, its condition looks equal to the previous two. *Dick Copello*

Bruck Brodbeck of Toledo, Ohio, restored this B-3 series Dodge cab-over-engine from 1953. *Dick Copello*

Another 1955 C-3 series Dodge was this one owned by Red Star Transit Company of Detroit, Michigan. The power in this tractor was a 331-ci V-8 engine. The open-top trailer was a Fruehauf. *Neil Sherff*

This 1954 C-1 series Dodge was owned by Kings Moving & Storage Company. This was one of the older-style straight truck furniture haulers. Kings were agents for United Van Lines, which was based in Fenton, Missouri. *George Fiebe*

Tom Oehme of Lititz, Pennsylvania, did a very fine restoration job on his 1955 C-3 series Dodge sleeper. A few little extras gave this Dodge the custom appearance. The rack side flatbed trailer matches the tractor's appearance nicely. *Dick Copello*

U.S.A.C. Transport Inc. of Detroit, Michigan, was a specified commodity carrier hauling a lot of government loads. The carrier used all owner-operator tractors like this 1957 D series Dodge. U.S.A.C. Transport was a 48-state carrier. *Neil Sherff*

This 1957 D series Dodge is unloading at the Lewter Pens located in Texas. The livestock trailer could be a Hobbs or a Hyde. The carrier is unknown. *Ron Adams Collection*

In this picture there are two sets of twins. Garrett Freight Lines of Pocatello, Idaho, had these two C series 1957 Dodge cab-over-engine tractors with two Williamsen 24-foot trailers doing pickup and delivery work in their city delivery fleet. *Garrett Freight Lines Inc.*

Another Model 900 Dodge for North American Van Lines of Fort Wayne, Indiana. *North American Van Lines*

Baker Driveaway Company of Detroit, Michigan, used this 1960 D series Dodge tractor to haul none other than Dodge cars. Back in this era, most of the car hauler trailers had closed sides. *Baker Driveaway Co.*

This 1959 NC900 Dodge and Trailmobile trailer were with North American Van Lines of Fort Wayne, Indiana. An NH-195 Cummins diesel kept this rig moving down the road. Notice this was the old North American paint scheme before they went to the red, white, and gold. The driver had the convenience of an add-on sleeper. *Neil Sherff*

Dodge changed their cab styles quite often through the 1950s. This NCT 900 model measured 89 inches from bumper to back of cab and featured a NH-180 Cummins diesel engine. The trailer is a late-1950s Fruehauf. *Ron Adams Collection*

CHAPTER 6

Ford Motor Company

If there was ever one man whose name stood out in the automotive field above the rest, it would have to be Henry Ford. He built his first commercial vehicle in 1905, at the age of 40. His first truck was a cargo box mounted on a Model C chassis. In 1908, the famous Model T was introduced. Although Ford did not make a truck chassis at this time, aftermarket conversions were fitted on the Model T chassis. The power came from a four-cylinder engine. By 1909, Ford was producing 100 per day.

In 1910, Ford moved to a new plant in Highland Park, Michigan, that ultimately employed 16,000 workers. Another new plant was opened in Kansas City, Missouri, and the total output was over 32,000 units. After a brief time away from truck manufacturing, Ford got back into it in 1917 on a permanent basis. The 2 millionth Model T was built in 1917, the same year that Henry Ford's first grandson was born, Henry Ford II. In 1923 there were over 193,000 truck chassis and 1.8 million Model T passenger cars. Ford started building their own truck bodies in 1924 and offered eight combinations of cabs and bodies. In 1925, Ford built its 1 millionth truck chassis and had manufactured 75 percent of all the trucks in the United States at this time.

Through the 1910s and 1920s, Ford acquired many businesses, leaving the company with a total of 86 plants. In November of 1927, a new Model AA was introduced and replaced the Model TT. In 1930, a new assembly plant was completed in Richmond, California. The Great Depression took its toll on car and truck production in 1931. Another model change took place in 1932 with the Model BB, and also the new 65-horsepower V-8 engine. The Repeal of the Volstead Act helped rejuvenate truck sales as the need arose to haul large legal quantities of alcoholic beverages. Third axles also became available. By 1935, all open cabs were phased out. By 1938, Ford had pulled ahead of the top-four truck manufacturers in sales, due in part to avoiding production disruptions from the labor strikes that hurt other manufacturers.

The truck models were restyled in 1938, the year of the first Ford-built cab-over-engine. Hydraulic brakes became standard on all Fords in 1939. At this time Grico built a twin-engine Ford tractor.

In February 1942, all civilian production was converted to military production. In 1944, the automotive industry was authorized to build 80,000 new commercial civilian trucks to prevent total fatigue of our nation's domestic transportation industry. As the war came to an end, all vehicle rationing was abolished. By 1947, Ford truck production reached over 5 million.

In 1948, Ford trucks took on a new look with the 115 body and chassis combination on the F-1 to F-8 and featured the new 145-horsepower 337-ci V-8 engine. The Korean War brought new demand for truck production because the American public anticipated rationing as in World War II. The F series trucks continued through the 1950s. The year 1956 saw construction start on 41,000 miles of the Interstate Highway System. The following year, 1957, saw the end of the old-style cab-over-engine, and a change to the new look of the flat-faced tilt-cab with set-back front axles, which was the new C series. In 1959, there were 370 different models of commercial vehicles. The Ford truck tractor packages were F-750 to F-1100, C-750 to C-1100, and T-850 and T-950.

Over the next few years, several new models were introduced, such as the N series. By 1963, Ford offered over 1,000 different truck models, both diesel and gas. In 1961, a new H series high cab-over-engine was introduced but was replaced by the W-1000 series in 1966, with GCW rated up to 80,000 pounds. The end of the 1960s decade yielded a new L series from the Louisville, Kentucky, plant. A total of 30 different gas and diesel engines up to 335 horsepower were offered along with 6- to 16-speed transmissions. In 1974, Ford was third in heavy truck sales, behind International and Mack. Over the next years a number of new models came on the scene. The CL cab-over-engine and the LTL conventional and the Aeromax took to the road.

In 1998, Freightliner Corporation took over the heavy-duty Ford truck line and renamed it Sterling, which brings back a name from many years before. Over the years, Ford has come a long way and it looks like they still have a long way to go.

Although this is not an over-the-road truck, it served its purpose as a local truck. Bremerton Ice & Fuel Company was the owner of this Ford F-6. *Ron Adams Collection*

This style Ford was started in 1948 and continued through 1950. Being a restored job, ownership of this truck is unknown. *Ron Adams Collection*

To bring home the bread was not the job of this Ford F-6, but to deliver the bread was its job. Protection gear (being the grille guard) was added to protect the grille on this 1951 Ford F-6. The graphics on the Utility trailer tell the whole story about the Oroweat product. *Utility Trailer Company*

This 1951 Ford F-8 V-8 was running over the road for Roadway Express of Akron, Ohio. Those famous colors of blue and orange could be seen almost anywhere in the eastern half of the United States. The trailer belonging to Roadway Express is a late-1940s Fruehauf Aero-Van. Notice the 1949 Ford car behind the truck. *Neil Sherff*

The cab-over-engine types were used for both over-the-road and local distribution. This 1952 Ford F-6 powered by a Ford V-8 engine did local beer distributing for the Rainier Brewing Company in Washington State. *Ron Adams Collection*

The cab-over-engine style changed somewhat from 1952 to 1953. The noticeable change is the grille style. This 1953 Ford "Big Job" cab-over-engine was hauling steel and metal products for Brada Cartage Company of Detroit, Michigan. This was the Midwest-type truck-trailer combination. *Neil Sherff*

The 1953 conventional tractor styling changed from the 1952 styling. The hood and grille were the main changes on this Ford F-750. The tractor and trailer were leased to Consolidated Lines of Saginaw, Michigan, hauling steel and metal products. *Neil Sherff*

The 1954 model stayed basically the same as the previous year with the exception of the grille. This Ford "Big Job" tractor was teamed up with a late-1940s Fruehauf Aero-Van. Fred V. Gentsch, makers of modern furniture and beds, was the owner. *Neil Sherff*

For the year 1955, we see another change in the grille styling. This Ford C-800 cab-over-engine tractor took its turn among the ranks hauling freight for Daniels Motor Freight of Warren, Ohio. *Neil Sherff*

Another cab-over-engine in 1955 was this Ford C-600 straight truck with a Clark body. It was part of the city delivery fleet for C.C.C. Highway. *C.C.C. Highway Inc.*

Another version of the cab-over-engine is this Ford C-750 J-8 powered straight truck. Course Manufacturing Company in Union, New Jersey, was most likely the builder of the body. *Ron Adams Collection*

The 1956 conventional models also got the new grille design. It is seen here either loading or delivering a brand-new set of Trailmobile flatbed trailers. This Ford F-800 looks good teamed up with the flatbeds. *Trailmobile Inc.*

Backed up to the dock getting loaded is this Ford F-800 tractor and Ohio trailer. The tractor was leased to Daniels Motor Freight of Warren, Ohio. *Neil Sherff*

This 1956 Ford F-800 tractor and unknown trailer owned by Barry Moore Haulage of Cooksville, Ontario, Canada, was photographed in 1987 at the American Truck Historical Society convention in Schaumburg, Illinois. A pretty nice restoration job. *Ron Adams Collection*

In 1957 Ford introduced its all-new tilt cab-over-engine series. The Red Star Transit Company in Detroit, Michigan, had some of them. The rag-top trailer is an early-1950s Fruehauf. *Neil Sherff*

In 1958, there was a whole new change in designing the new Ford conventional tractors. Dual headlights, grated grille, and three holes were part of the new design. Earl C. Smith in Port Huron, Michigan, had several, one teamed up with an early-1950s Fruehauf trailer. *Neil Sherff*

At this time, there were many F series Fords on the road by both companies and owner-operators. This one was in the fleet for Middle Atlantic Transportation Company of Bridgeport, Connecticut. It is paired up with an early-1950s Fruehauf open-top trailer. *Neil Sherff*

In 1957 Ford came out with their new tilt-cab C series cab-over-engine. The type was used for both city and local deliveries and also over-the-road trucking. This C-600 was owned by Ronald Sinclair, who leased his tractor to Mayflower Transit Company of Indianapolis, Indiana, pulling one of the company's Trailmobile trailers hauling household goods nationwide. *Mayflower Transit Co.*

The C series was offered in many variations. Jerseymaid, a California-based company, owned this C-600 tandem-axle Ford tractor and SWX Model 500 Utility reefer van in 1958. The Utility trailer was 35 feet long and had sliding curbside doors. *Utility Trailer Co.*

CHAPTER 7

White-Freightliner

Tire shop owner Leland James didn't pick the most auspicious time to start Freightways, given that the stock market crash kicked off the depression in October the same year, 1929. Nonetheless, the Portland, Oregon, trucking company survived, and later merged with others to become Consolidated Freightways.

Unable to find a durable lightweight truck that met his needs, James hired engineers to design his own, and set up his shop and terminal in Salt Lake City, Utah, to build them. Their first experimental cab was mounted on a Fageol chassis and powered by a Cummins diesel. After further experiments, they came up with a successful new design that they called the Freightway, which was later changed to Freightliner.

World War II interrupted the plans of the newly named Freightliner Corporation, and they converted to make airplane parts and ship hatch covers. Following the war, after being charged by the U.S. Justice Department of having a monopoly in 48 states, the Salt Lake City shop was closed. All equipment and materials were moved to Portland, Oregon, where a new Freightliner Corporation was formed. Early Freightliners were built for Consolidated Freightways, use only, but by 1948 they were selling trucks to outside customers.

The design of the Freightliner was known as the "Bubblenose." This was the model WF800, which was a day cab. In 1950, the Model WF900 was introduced, which was an integral sleeper cab. In 1951, Freightliner signed a 25-year agreement with the White Motor Company to market, sell, and service Freightliner trucks at the White dealer service branches. They then became known as White-Freightliner. Production increased tremendously because of White advertising White-Freightliner trucks. In 1952, they introduced a new flat-front cab. Freightliner also designed a new 48-inch cab, which accommodated a rooftop sleeper.

Freightliners were powered by the "Pancake" Cummins diesel engine. The cab had three removable panels for access to the engine. The 48-inch cab allowed for more cargo space. In 1958, Freightliner introduced their first tilt-cab. It tilted to a full 90 degrees. The new designs led to increased sales, and a new plant was started in Pomona, California, to increase production. Total production in 1961

reached 1,242 trucks, and the same year Freightliner started manufacturing in Canada. By 1963, the 10,000th Freightliner was built.

Around this time, half-cab Freightliners were made for the construction industry. Freightliner truck sales were up to 4,768 by 1965. A new plant was built in Indianapolis, Indiana, to make the COE trucks, and the Portland, Oregon, plant was converted to parts and warehousing. In 1968, Freightliner came out with another first in the industry: a 104-inch cab known as the Vanliner. In 1973, the Powerliner was introduced; it had a larger grille to accommodate engines of 500 or more horsepower. A new lightweight conventional tractor was also introduced that year. But 1975 proved to be a disastrous year for all Class 8 trucks because of fuel shortages, rationing, and raised fuel prices. The 25-year sales agreement between Freightliner and the White Motor Company expired.

In 1979, another new plant was opened in Mt. Holly, North Carolina. A 60-inch raised roof sleeper was offered as optional equipment. In 1981, Freightliner was purchased by Daimler-Benz for $260 million. In 1986, Freightliner introduced the Hard Hat series for the construction industry. In 1996 Freightliner added more to their line of products with the purchase of the American LaFrance Company

Even though Freightliner is not as old a manufacturer as a lot of others, they have come a long way and have offered to the industry many new products.

This was Freightliner's first style cab, the "Bubblenose." Although the trucking company is unknown, the Montana license plate was from 1950.
Ron Adams Collection

This fresh-off-the-line 1951 model is wearing the new White-Freightliner nameplate. This came about when Freightliner and the White Motor Company signed a 25-year contract to market and service Freightliner trucks and the White service centers. *Freightliner Corp.*

Freightliner was the first to have a 48-inch cab. This gave the company the opportunity to pull longer trailers or for longer bodies on truck-trailer units. The Bubblenose was not that short but one of the shortest cab-over day cabs at the time. The White-Freightliner and Fruehauf double trailers were owned by So-Cal Freight Lines of Palo Alto, California. *Freightliner Corp.*

Double trailers came in almost every type. This unknown brand of double-hopper trailers was pulled by a single-axle White-Freightliner tractor. Direct Delivery System was the owner of the outfit in 1953. *Freightliner Corp.*

Sleeper cabs were a must for a lot of long-distance truckers. Although this is not a sleeper cab, it is sleeper equipped. On truck-trailer combinations sleeper cabs were available, but if you got a sleeper cab, this meant a shorter body with less payload. To overcome that problem a sleeper compartment was offered in the front of the body, as seen here. Warren Davis of Portland, Oregon, had his White-Freightliner with Fruehauf body and Utility trailer set up that way. *Ron Adams Collection*

Another truck-trailer combination on this White-Freightliner is a tanker for Cantlay & Tanzola Transportation Company of Los Angeles, California. The capacity of the tank body was 3,500 gallons and the capacity of the trailer was 4,400 gallons. *Cantlay & Tanzola Inc.*

Long-wheelbase tractors were common on Western highways. Some carriers utilized the extra space between the cab and trailer by placing a Dromedary body on the frame for extra payload. The White-Freightliner tractor and Trailmobile trailer could have been owned by Salt Lake–Knabb Freight Lines. *Ron Adams Collection*

A long-wheelbase tractor with a sleeper cab and no Dromedary was owned by Asbury–Arrowhead Freight Lines of Los Angeles, California, and Salt Lake City, Utah. Dry freight was being loaded in the Fruehauf stainless steel trailer. *Freightliner Corp.*

Some long-wheelbase tractors were almost as long as the trailers they pulled. Freightliner offered wheelbases anywhere from approximately 131 inches up to 250–260 inches. St. Johns Motor Express of Portland, Oregon, had various types of equipment for hauling liquid commodities and heavy equipment. St. Johns was later taken over by Widing Transportation Company, also of Portland, Oregon. *Ron Adams Collection*

St. Johns Motor Express of Portland, Oregon, used this White-Freightliner tractor in their heavy hauling operation. Notice that the cab has no sleeper, but an add-on sleeper box. The cargo is a Plymouth switch locomotive used for switching cars in a railroad yard. *Freightliner Corp.*

Livestock haulers were also among the White-Freightliner users. A. J. Bone of Broadus, Montana, selected this WF64T to pull his Wilson straight floor livestock trailer. Notice on the trailer the old, simple three-digit phone number. *Freightliner Corp.*

We saw the old-style cab with the high-rise sleeper, now we see the new-style cab with the high-rise sleeper. This model was a WF4864DD with a Cummins NHHT horizontal diesel engine. The 48-inch cab allowed mounting an 8-foot Dromedary body behind the cab, pulling a 35-foot trailer, while staying within the 50-foot length. The tractor was engineered for Ringsby Truck Lines of Denver, Colorado. *Freightliner Corp.*

A truck-trailer combination was a typical Western truck, used in several different variations. Susanville Van Storage and Freight Company of Susanville, California, chose a flatbed combination for the type of hauling that they had to do. Their choice was a White-Freightliner. *Brian Williams*

With truck-trailer combinations, the shorter the cab, the bigger the body, the more cargo could be hauled. Such was the case with Garibaldi Bros. of Los Angeles, California. This 1955 White-Freightliner Model 4864, which had the 48-inch "Pancake" cab, allowed for more cargo space. In this case, the extra space was used for one or two more head of cattle. The body and trailer brand are unknown. *Freightliner Corp.*

Lee & Eastes of Seattle, Washington, wanted to maximize the payload. To accomplish that, some special engineering and designing were done whereby the cab was shortened 48 inches and a 180- or 200-horsepower Pancake Cummins diesel engine was installed. Notice the short grille and left side mounted stack. The body and trailer were designed by Brown Trailer Company. *Freightliner Corp.*

Another Lee & Eastes truck was this White-Freightliner WF4864H with Dromedary body. The long wheelbase allows for more cargo space. This unit also had a left side mounted stack. The unknown-brand-name trailer was owned by U and I Sugar Company. *Freightliner Corp.*

White-Freightliners were frequently used in hauling for the agricultural business. Shirley Robertson of Chowchilla, California, had his circa-1958 White-Freightliner and double trailers hauling baled hay to some feedlot in California. *Brian Williams*

As 40-foot trailers were becoming legal, tractors had to be engineered to pull these trailers and stay within the 50-foot legal limit, especially in the eastern and midwestern states. Consolidated Freightways of Menlo Park, California, used a 48-inch cab to overcome that. The louvers behind the cab door were probably needed to help cool the engine. The trailer was made by Miller Trailers of Bradenton, Florida. *Consolidated Freightways Inc.*

Double trailers were also a part of the family of Western-type equipment. The White-Freightliner tractor and Fruehauf trailers saw many miles up and down the Pacific Coast. This sleeper cab also had the side louvers to help cool the engine.
Los Angeles–Seattle Motor Express

These tractors are part of a fleet replacement for Western-Gillette Transport of Los Angeles, California. The tractors are powered by a NHB Cummins diesel engine. Each tractor has a 234-inch wheelbase and would probably take on a Dromedary body. Western-Gillette routes went from San Francisco and Los Angeles through Arizona, New Mexico, Texas, Oklahoma, and up to Kansas City. *Freightliner Corp.*

Another well-known user of Freightliner trucks is Navajo Freight Lines of Denver, Colorado. Navajo used these Dromedary rigs in the western part of their operations due to length laws. The wheelbase could be as long as 240 inches. Notice that on the side of the trailer you will see Albuquerque, New Mexico. This was their main office before they moved it to Denver, Colorado. *Navajo Freight Lines Inc.*

Lloyd Morrison of Salina, Kansas, used his circa-1959 White-Freightliner and Trail-Liner livestock trailer to haul livestock in the prairie states, the West, and Southwest. The compartments underneath the trailer were probably for the side panels that slid in between the exterior posts to keep out the cold weather so that the cattle didn't freeze in the winter months. *Ron Adams Collection*

General Motors Truck Company

In 1911, William Durant formed the General Motors Truck Company, or GMC, out of several smaller truck builders he had acquired previously. In 1912, early GMCs came equipped with a 40-horsepower four-cylinder engine. Electric trucks were also built at this time. In 1916, GM staged a cross-country trip from Seattle to New York City in 31 days by driver Williams Warwick and his wife with a load of Carnation milk on a GMC truck.

After producing about 21,000 trucks for the war, GMC sold many different models in different weight classes through the 1920s. In the 1930s, the company began building bigger trucks up to 15-ton capacity with sleeper cabs, and styling was influenced by the aerodynamic streamlining trend. In 1937, GMC offered 12 conventional models ranging from 1/2-ton to 10-ton, and 11 cab-over-engine models up to 12-ton. Sales topped 50,000 units.

As World War II began, GMC quickly converted to military production. There were five 6x6 versions, and 1942 saw GMC produce 148,111 units. In 1943, GMC built 16 different types of trucks for the military. After the war, GMC started building trucks for commercial use again. By 1950, GMC had 20 improved models from 1/2-ton up to 20-ton. In mid-1950, GMC introduced a new 110-inch six-cylinder, 275-horsepower diesel engine and later that year broke civilian production records when its 100,000th truck came off the line, a 650 diesel. GMC also had a 953 diesel highway tractor with 200 horsepower and a GCW rating of 70,000 pounds. In August 1954, GMC introduced its Stripaway cab-over-engine system, which allowed better, quicker, and easier access to the engine, transmission, and other components, and included a counterbalanced slide-up seat, fold-back floorboards, and swing-out side doors on each side of the hood. By 1955, 65 models used automatic transmissions. In 1959, GMC brought out a new set of engines, including three V-6s and one V-12. GMC was also selling a 48-inch BBC tractor Model DFR-8000, which had a 50-inch front-axle setback.

The late 1950s and early 1960s saw restyling of the cabs. The D series cab-over-engine was available in day cab or in sleeper cabs. In the later 1960s, the all-new restyled Astro 95 cab-over-engine was introduced along with the 9500 series conventional that came in either a long hood or a short hood. In the later 1970s, the General made its appearance, followed by the Brigadier. Several different engines were offered in these models. In 1982, the COE Astro 95 all had turbocharged after-cooled engines. That same year, aerodynamics came into the picture and the Astro 95 was fitted with a roof-mounted air deflector, which was called the Drag Foiler. This pattern followed with all the heavy-duty models. And then in January 1988, the big merger between GMC and Volvo White took place. The new name was Volvo White/GMC.

Every truck and trailer manufacturer has had a Hollywood star involved with their product at one time or another. In this case, the circa-1950 GMC tractor and Nabors Trailer belonged to old-time Western star Wild Bill Elliot, standing on the ramp. The rig was used for transporting Elliot's horse and all his tack for making Western movies. *Nabors Trailers*

This style GMC was made from 1948 to 1953. March 2, 1957, was picture day for GMC number 396, owned by Jacobs Transfer Company of Baltimore, Maryland. Jacobs also had straight trucks in their city delivery fleet with the same cab and hood style. Notice Jacob's version of a grille guard. *Jacobs Transfer Co.*

Some straight trucks were also considered over-the-road big rigs. Straight trucks such as this GMC with Black Diamond body were used for hauling new furniture from factory to show room. Most furniture bodies were closed-top, but this one is an open-top. *Black Diamond Trailer Co.*

Most of the truck-trailer combinations that ran in the Western states were tandem-axle trucks, but some single-axles were in existence. F-D-S Manufacturing Company had this GMC gas job from the early 1950s working for them. Notice that the truck body and trailer had about a 12-inch extension added to them to make the body and trailer higher. *Stan Holtzman*

This picture was taken in 1972 at the Bartonsville 76 Truck Stop in Bartonsville, Pennsylvania. This older GMC had the long wheelbase, which was rarely seen in the East at this time. K&J Produce Company of Pensacola, Florida, must have been proud to have this circa-1952–1953 GMC hauling for them along with the Utility reefer trailer. *Ron Adams*

McLean Trucking Company of Winston-Salem, North Carolina, was always a big user of GMC trucks. Here we see a fleet of at least 29 GMC 650 diesels with integral sleepers. McLean used these on the north-south runs from the Carolinas to the Philadelphia and New York City areas. *McLean Trucking*

This picture was taken in the Camden, New Jersey, area in 1957. Notice the extended bumper and hood that were probably modified to accommodate a bigger engine. The GMC diesel had an add-on box sleeper and was pulling a Trailmobile reefer trailer. The owner and company are unknown. *Bob Parrish*

March 1, 1958, was picture day for this GMC 850 diesel and Utility LSM-15 low-bed trailer owned by L. C. Anderson Company contractors. The load is a TD-24 Dozer and Ateco Ripper. The trailer has been cleared for 110,000 pounds gross on a California purple-rated highway for Western Truck Lines. Notice the Sterling tractor behind the low-bed trailer. *Utility Trailers – Fresno Branch*

The Richfield Oil Company in California had a sizeable fleet of trucks. One of those trucks was this GMC 750 gas-powered cab-over-engine, pulling a Fruehauf gasoline tank trailer. The Richfield colors were blue and yellow. *Ron Adams Collection*

Here we have another GMC fleet shot from 1953. Akers Motor Lines of Gastonia, North Carolina, another Southern-based carrier, is the owner of this fleet of GMC sleeper cab diesels. These "Cannonball" GMC trucks could be seen running along the East Coast routes from the Carolinas up into New York and New England. *GMC Truck & Coach*

One of the most famous trucks of the 1950s was the "Cannonball" GMC. Many of them were made, but over the years a lot of them seemed to find their way to the junkyards after their life ended. Thanks to Don Rogers of Whitby, Ontario, Canada, this 1954 950 GMC diesel was revived with a new life. Rogers' restoration made it look better than new. The Great Dane produce trailer is the perfect partner for this tractor. *Bob Baciulis*

This owner-operated Model 870 sleeper leased to Hess Cartage Company of Melvindale, Michigan, was another Cannonball GMC diesel. Though truck-trailer combinations were usually found in the West, Michigan and Ohio also had a few of these combinations running the highways in that area. Steel products seem to be the "undercover" load for this trip. *Neil Sherff*

A Euclid earthmover was the load on this trip. Curtis Keal Transport Company of Cleveland, Ohio, had the honors of doing the job. A GMC gas job with a day cab was the power source for the transit. *Curtis Keal Transport Co.*

In 1958 GMC restyled their conventional tractor. This GMC 860 was used in many different applications. Here we see an 860 as a tandem-axle tractor with an integral sleeper cab. It probably had a 189-horsepower GMC diesel engine. Daniels Motor Freight of Warren, Ohio, used this one for their general freight hauling. *Neil Sherff*

R. W. Express of Dearborn, Michigan, used this 1958–1959 GMC 860 and an unknown-brand rack side trailer for hauling steel and metal products in the Midwest. *Neil Sherff*

GMC produced more than 141,000 trucks in 1958–1959, among them this 860 diesel. The driver added dual air horns and stacks along with an add-on sleeper box for a slightly custom look. Allen Canning Company of Siloam Springs, Arkansas, was the owner of this GMC 860 and late-1940s-era Fruehauf Aero-Van trailer. *Neil Sherff*

The late 1950s was the start of the D series GMC. This model carried through to 1968. This sleeper cab version was leased to Bekins Van Lines of Omaha, Nebraska, to haul household goods cross-country in the Aluminum Body Company trailer. *Detroit Diesel*

Many railroads had their own truck fleets. This D series GMC was powered by a V-8 Detroit Diesel engine to pull the Utility trailer load of freight for Southern Pacific Truck Service, the trucking division of the Southern Pacific Railroad. *Southern Pacific*

The D series GMC was becoming very popular, not only with the trucking companies, but also the private carriers such as Air Reduction Company in Detroit, Michigan. It had a day cab and was powered by a V-8 Detroit Diesel engine. *Detroit Diesel*

International Harvester Company

Cyrus McCormick invented grain reapers in 1831 and specialized in farm equipment throughout the 1800s. McCormick produced its first tractor in 1889, and built what were known as Auto Buggies in 1902—though actual production did not start until 1907. In October of that same year, the Auto Buggy Manufacturing facilities were moved to Akron, Ohio. The 1912 models were the first to carry the International Harvester Company (IHC) insignia and a letter, Model A or Model M.

In 1915, truck production began with five new models, H, F, K, G and L, ranging from 3/4-ton to 3-ton capacity. The Renault-type hood was used on each model, with the radiator behind the engine. The models H and L would be discontinued in 1923. A new plant was built in Springfield, Ohio, and 7,000 trucks were built in 1921. By the time of the stock market crash in 1929, they had 170 branches and were producing 50,000 trucks a year. The A series was a new model made from 1929 to 1934, and there were major styling changes in 1930. They started making their own diesel engines in 1933.

The new C series was introduced in 1934 and was in production until 1937, with 18 different models, from 1/2-ton to 7-ton capacity. The six-wheelers were designed in 1935. In 1936, International introduced the C-300 cab-over-engine, followed by a new, redesigned truck known as the D series in 1937. At this time, the lineup consisted of 25 overlapping models and production topped 100,000 units for the first time. A new sleeper cab was developed in 1938, and by this time, International had built over 1 million trucks. The company ranked third in production.

The D series was phased out with the introduction of the new K series in 1940. During World War II, International produced more than 100,000 units for the military. After the war, the K line was continued as the KB, which had a wider grille. In 1947, production of the Western trucks and the new W series International Western started at International's new Emeryville, California, plant. Two gasoline and three diesel engines were available for the new W series.

In 1950, the KB series was phased out and replaced with the new L series that had the headlights mounted in the fender instead of on the fender. A new COE Emeryville, known as the LDC-400, was introduced in 1950 and could pull a 35-foot trailer legally anywhere in the United States. The standard engine was a Cummins, but Buda and Hall-Scott were optional. The conventional partner to the LDC-400 COE was the LD-400, which replaced the W series. In 1953, the L series became the R series. Many of these cab styles were used through the 1950s. The R series cab-over-engine was replaced with a newly designed flat-front cab-over known as the DCO-405. The V series and A series were two popular models. Through the 1950s, there were about 15 different styles of trucks, which carried over into the 1960s.

In 1963, two new models made their appearance, the DC-400 Transtar and the Fleetstar, which later replaced the R series. The new CO4000 cab-over-engine made its debut in 1965, replacing the DCO Emeryville. In the later 1960s, the Stars arrived, including the Transtar, Transtar II, Paystar, Cargostar, and Transtar 4300, along with the Loadstar. All kinds of engines and transmissions were offered in these series.

The F series conventional and the CO-9670 were International's most popular models through the 1980s, when aerodynamics became part of the dress code on International trucks.

In late 1949, the L series was introduced. This L-170 or L-180 tractor and Trailmobile trailer was owned by Blue-Arrow Transport Lines of Grand Rapids, Michigan. This model used International's Super Blue Diamond engine, which put out 100 horsepower with a four- or five-speed transmission.
Ron Adams Collection

There were many variations in the L series of the bigger style. One variation from the L-170 or L-180 was that the hood was a lot higher due to the use of a bigger engine. This L series, an L-185 or higher, and Andrews TA-32 van belonged to Mound City Forwarding Company of St. Louis, Missouri, which operated in both Missouri and Illinois. *Andrews Trailers*

The LD-300, which featured the set-back front axle, was also designated the Diesel series. This LD-305 was powered by a Cummins diesel, probably the HRB-600. Spector Motor Service of Chicago, Illinois, put this one to work on their routes from the Midwest to the East Coast. *Spector Motor Service*

The cab-over-engine version of the L series was the LDC-400. This COE model, like most others of this time, was the snub-nose type. This was also one of the Emeryville group. J. E. Down was the owner of the rig with an unknown brand-name trailer. A Cummins HRB-600 diesel engine was standard on this model with Hall-Scott and Buda engines optional. *Ron Adams Collection*

Another one of the big boys from International was this LDF-400 with the integral sleeper cab. Like the cab-over-engine model, this one was also probably powered by a Cummins HRB-600 diesel engine. The Hall-Scott and Buda engines were optional equipment. *I.H.C.*

The L series ran for four years but was replaced by the R series in 1953. The new R series was basically the same appearance and style as the previous L series, but with a different style grille. Northwestern Glass Company of Seattle, Washington, used this Model R170-180 to pull the late-1940s Fruehauf trailer. *Ron Adams Collection*

The R series was basically the same as the previous L series, with the change in the grille being from seven bars in the grille on the L series to three bars on the R series. The R-205 Roadliner sleeper cab was teamed up with a Trailmobile tank trailer. A Buda or Cummins diesel were the power choices. Notice how the smokestack in the background looks like it might be the diesel stack on the tractor. *I.H.C.*

The RDs were used in all modes of hauling. This one hauled produce from South to North with a Great Dane trailer for Rismiller Transportation of Leesburg, Florida. A Cummins diesel was the source of power. *Joe Wanchura*

American Mineral Spirits Company had this R-200 International and Fruehauf rack side trailer hauling their own products. The R-200 was one of the more popular models in the R series. *Ron Adams Collection*

In 1954, Pacific Intermountain Express of Oakland, California, purchased a large fleet of these RDC-405 tractors. They were used mainly between Denver and Chicago, and were capable of pulling 35-foot trailers. The power came from a JT-6 Cummins diesel engine. Sleeper teams were used on this run. *PIE*

In 1955 another new model, the CO series, appeared. This Model 200 was owned by Ellsworth Freight Lines of Eagle Grove, Iowa, as were the Fruehauf reefer trailers. Hauling refrigerated products was the main business for this company. *Ron Adams Collection*

The D series cab-over-engine was still a very popular truck during the early 1950s. This DTC-405 was owned by Vern Hartley of Sacramento, California. This somewhat long wheelbase was one of the many configurations available in this D series. A 40-foot Pike trailer with a West Coast tandem setting matches nicely with the tractor. *Brian Williams*

This truck-trailer combination owned by the El Monte Hay Market of El Monte, California, was another DTC-405. Rigs of this type were common in the western states. All types of bodies with matching trailers were available for different types of hauling. *Brian Williams*

This Western International was the third generation of the W series of the later 1940s. The 1955 RDF-405 International was returned to life by Gary Johnson of Princeton, Illinois. *Don MacKenzie*

In 1956 another new line joined the International family, the V series. This fleet of V-190 tractors and Trailmobile trailers was owned by Western Auto Supply Company at the Houston, Texas, branch. The two tractors in the distance are AC models, which came out in 1957. *Lloyd Koenig Studios*

Rarely seen in the R line was the RD series, the D referring to diesel. This R-200 diesel is powered by a Cummins ST-6-B diesel engine. This model was the Super Space Saver. Four inches were removed from the back of the cab, and the cab was moved forward 4 inches. The front bumper was moved back 4 inches. The front axle moved forward by 2 inches. The total BBC (bumper to back of cab) length-savings was 12 inches. Campbells 66 Express of Springfield, Missouri, liked the engineering enough to buy several of them to pull this Trailmobile 40-foot open-top trailer. *Campbells 66 Express Inc.*

In 1954, when the new CO series was introduced, the standard engine was the Super Red Diamond 372 engine. In 1956, they introduced the V-8 engine, making it a VCO. This Model VCO International and Kentucky moving van was owned by Richardson Moving & Storage Company of Salina, Kansas. *Richardson Moving & Storage*

This DFC-405-L International was Cummins powered. Hall-Scott gas engines were also offered as an option. The tractor and 40-foot Brown trailer were owned by the Santa Fe Trail Transportation Company of Wichita, Kansas. This company was the Highway Division of the Santa Fe Railroad. *Santa Fe Trail Transportation Co. Inc.*

Truck-trailer combinations like this one were very popular in the West. This DFC-405 International was a livestock combination that was owned by Marlin Whittington of El Centro, California. The year 1956 could have been the last in which this style cab-over-engine was made. *Ron Adams Collection*

The famous DCO-405 Emeryville was born in 1956, replacing the DFC model. Many companies used these cab-over-engines and Navajo Freight Lines of Denver, Colorado, was no exception. It was Cummins powered, but all the optional engines offered were Cummins, from 165 up to 335 horsepower. At this time Navajo operated through the Southwest, north to Denver and east to Chicago. *International Harvester Co.*

This DCOT-405 was Unit No. 8 for Golden State Rodeo Ranch of Brawley, California. A Brown trailer was used to transport the rodeo cattle. This style Emeryville cab was made for 11 years. This one is Cummins powered, but later on, around 1964, Detroit and Caterpillar diesel engines were offered. *Brian Williams*

International Transport of Rochester, Minnesota, was a heavy-hauling carrier that had a variety of different equipment in their fleet. In the late 1950s, Internationals such as this DCOT-405 seemed to be plentiful in this fleet. Bulldozers, like these two Caterpillars, were a regular commodity for this transcontinental carrier. *International Transport*

Another new cab-over-engine in the International line of trucks was the ACO series in 1957. This one was most likely a 1958 since that was the first year a sleeper cab was offered on this model. It was known as the "SightLiner." Four V series engines were offered on this model. Fred's Truck Line of Arapahoe, Nebraska, owned this one to pull a 40-foot Wilson livestock trailer. *Wilson Trailer Co.*

Although the year on this truck is 1960 or 1961, this BC series was introduced in 1959. Deaton Truck Lines of Birmingham, Alabama, owned this BC-220 International, which was pulling a dump trailer on this run. This BC series was phased out after being made for only three years, 1959–1961. *Deaton Truck Lines Inc.*

The RDF-400 Conventional series came to an end in 1961. Nevada Sales and Service of Las Vegas, Nevada, teamed this tractor to a Utility reefer trailer. Long-wheelbase tractors like this one were very popular in the Western states. *Brian Williams*

The International RDF series was a popular conventional truck with a good number of Western carriers and owner-operators. This unknown owner-operator added a few extras like an extra stack, add-on sleeper box, flying-swan hood ornament, and two mirrors to give it the custom look. This RDF model was teamed up to a grain trailer. *Brian Williams*

CHAPTER 10

Kenworth Truck Company

The beginnings of Kenworth trace back to 1915 when Louis Gerlinger and two sons, George and Louis Jr., started the Gerlinger Motor Car Company in Portland, Oregon. Soon after, a third son, Edward, also joined the company. The company initially sold Federal, Standard, and Menominee trucks, then started building their own trucks and came up with the name Gersix Manufacturing. The designer of the six-cylinder truck was George Peters. As the next few trucks were made, Buda and Wisconsin engines were used.

After only three years Gersix went bankrupt, and ended up under new owners, Edger Worthington and Fredrick Keen. The Portland plant was closed and Gersix Manufacturing Company moved to Seattle. They started making their own casting and metal components, but production was limited to one truck per month and totaled only 100 overall. Keen sold his interest in late 1922 to Harry Kent, who planned to build Kenworth trucks. The first of the custom-built Kenworth trucks, powered by Buda engines, came off the line in 1924. The depression years saw Kenworth introduce six-wheeled trucks and fire engines. In 1933, Kenworth sold its first sleeper cab truck. The first Bubblenose cab-over-engine model was unveiled in 1936, and by 1940 they produced 226 units for the year.

In 1941, the world's first aluminum diesel engine was built by Cummins and installed in a Kenworth. After the bombing of Pearl Harbor, Kenworth received a contract from the government to build 430 4-ton heavy-duty wrecker trucks for the military. Another 1,500 were ordered. They were all six-wheel drive and were equipped with all the necessary features for the job. Production of civilian trucks was down to 87 in 1943. In 1944, Kenworth was purchased by Pacific Car and Foundry Company.

When the war was over, Kenworth went back to normal production with a total of 705 trucks in 1946. As of 1950, 40 percent of Kenworth production was sold overseas. Also, the new flat-faced K series was introduced. In 1951, 1,700 Model 853s were made for the Arabian Oil Company. In 1952, yearly production passed the 1,000-unit mark. The cab-over-engine models were in high demand. In 1953, Kenworth introduced its new cab-beside-engine model. Almost all were made as truck tractors, and sleeper facilities were offered behind the engine.

The first four-axle Dromedary units were introduced in 1956 for Pacific Intermountain Express (PIE). Oil exploration in the Yukon Territory brought a fleet of Kenworth Model 923s that were powered by Cummins NH 200 diesel engines that worked 24 hours a day without switching off the engines in temperatures dipping to minus 60. The first full-tilt cab-over-engine was built in 1957.

Kenworth was mainly a Western-selling truck, but because of good sales in the eastern United States, a new factory was built in Kansas City, Missouri, in 1961. The famous W900 conventional and the K100 cab-over-engine were introduced in 1961. In 1966, record sales for that year totaled 3,900 trucks. A new plant was opened in Melbourne, Australia, and in 1974 another new plant opened in Chillicothe, Ohio, bringing production capacity to 16,000 trucks per year. From this point on, Kenworth prospered, offering some new models and improving what they had. New models included the Brute, Aerodyne, VIT, T600, and the latest, the T2000. Kenworth has come a long way and has lived up to the slogan of many years ago, "There's More Worth In Kenworth."

In the 1930s Kenworth came out with a cab-over-engine model known as the "Bubblenose." From the restyling of the cab came the ever-so-famous cab known as the "Bullnose." This style started around 1949–1950. This 1950 version was decked out with a Utility body and Utility pull trailer. Notice that Kenworth was still the nameplate before the individual letters. *Utility Trailer Co.*

This 1952 version of the Bullnose is a Model 825 C owned by Jim Dobbas of New Castle, California. Like many other models, the Bullnose was available in different variations. This truck-trailer combination was for hauling livestock. Notice that Kenworth was by then in individual letters. *Don MacKenzie*

One of the best-known reefer haulers in the 1950s, from Chicago to the West Coast, was Midwest Coast Transport of Sioux Falls, South Dakota. Although they were lease operators, like Hetrich Brothers of Minneapolis, Minnesota, there was a great collection of custom and colorful trucks. This Bullnose's colors are black and green with a white stripe. A mixed bag of reefer trailers was also among the fleet, such as this Aero-Liner. *Ron Adams Collection*

Kenworth trucks worked in all different fields and pulled every type of trailer. This outfit was pulling a set of cement hoppers for Superlite Rocks and Bricks. Notice the paint scheme where the right half of the tractor and trailers was a darker color than the left side. *McLaughlin & Co.*

In 1953, the cab-beside-engine model was introduced. It was available in a day cab or with a sleeper berth behind the driver and the engine. Weight was reduced by eliminating the right top half of the cab. From the looks of it, this one was joining the fleet of the Denver-Chicago Trucking Company. *Kenworth*

Double trailers were popular in the Western states. Portland-Seattle Auto Freight of Seattle, Washington, was one of the many Western carriers that used them. The Bullnose day cab and Brown trailers did their job with flying colors. *Ron Adams Collection*

Truck-trailer combinations were also used a lot on conventional trucks such as this Kenworth. They came in all forms and this one is a gasoline set. The tanks are of an unknown brand and new right from the manufacturer. *Ron Adams Collection*

Another form of a truck-trailer was a flatbed. Mixed lumber was the load on this trip for Hamman Lumber Company in Phoenix, Arizona. In this case, a sleeper box was added as an option. *Ron Adams Collection*

A mixed load of freight is the cargo on this trip. The Bullnose Kenworth and flatbed trailer are hauling for West Coast Equipment Company of Oakland, California. The pay for the freight on the Dromedary body was probably enough to cover the expenses on this trip, while the pay for the freight on the trailer was profit to the owner of the truck.
Ron Adams Collection

Kenworth made big trucks but they also made some bigger. As we see here, this is not an ordinary everyday truck. This is an oil field rigging unit that was used in the desert oil fields in the Mideast. Mobil Oil Company was the owner of this "Big Rig." *Kenworth*

This was Kenworth's first design for the flat-front cab-over-engine model. Notice the air scoops on the left and right front sides of the cab. The owner of the truck and Aero-Liner body and trailer was M. McGuire of Yakima, Washington. Also notice the small doors on the body and trailer. In some cases these were probably used as sleeper compartments. *Aero-Liner Corp.*

Another cab of the same style was this one for Arlington Cattle Company. The trailers are Fruehauf tanker-livestock combinations. Notice how the rear of the cab had a slight slant from bottom to top. *Kenworth*

A lot of Western conventional tractors had long wheelbases like this one. United States Express was the owner of the Kenworth tractor and flatbed trailer. Two Caterpillar industrial diesel engines were the load on this trip. Ron *Adams Collection*

The cab-beside-engine model was popular with some carriers. They were made for about 9 or 10 years. Merchants Freight System of St. Paul, Minnesota, used this no-sleeper model and Andrews reefer trailer as one of the fleet. *Fuller Manufacturing*

These Kenworth conventionals seemed to be the most popular truck in the Western states. Many trucking companies had them in their fleets, along with private carriers like West Coast Grocery Company. The frame-mounted fuel tanks were most of the time common on trucks that ran up to Alaska. This tractor looks good teamed to the Brown trailer. *Ron Adams Collection*

This first style flat-front cab-over-engine did have a couple of modifications. The headlights were recessed, the cab was square instead of the slight slant, and the windshield had an added wraparound corner piece on each side. The Kenworth with an Aero-Liner Dromedary body and Utility rack side trailer was owned by Consolidated Copperstate Lines. *Ron Adams Collection*

Here we have the same style cab but in a sleeper version. Los Angeles–Seattle Motor Express of Seattle, Washington, had this one hooked to a set of doubles to run up and down the Pacific Coast from Washington to California. *LASME*

Kenworths have always been the favorite truck to fancy up by the drivers. Dual chrome stacks, dual air horns, and a two- or three-tone color scheme seemed to be the popular items. Hill's Trucking added an aluminum sleeper box and pulled a 40-foot Pike reefer trailer. A Cummins diesel was the power source for this two-tone blue-and-white Kenworth. *Ron Adams Collection*

The Western owner-operators were big fans of the Kenworth conventional of this era. The optional extras that were added made this tractor look extra sharp. The big sleeper boxes were somewhat common in the Western states. A Cummins diesel engine was the power source for the tractor to pull the Pike reefer trailer. *Brian Williams*

The style of the narrow radiator still existed into the early 1960s. This late-1950s style sees the redesign of the fenders and adds dual headlights. The butterfly hood stayed through the 1950s. The truck-trailer propane tanker setup belongs to Dane Butane based in California. *Ron Adams Collection*

This slightly restyled cab-over-engine carried over into the 1960s. This 1958 model was owned by the Seattle Packing Company of Seattle, Washington, hauling cattle in this truck-trailer livestock combination. *Kenworth*

CHAPTER 11

Mack Trucks

In the 100-year history of commercial vehicles, no truck has made as big a hit as the Mack. It all started in 1901 in New York City with the five Mack brothers. Their first venture was a 15-passenger sightseeing bus. The success of that venture led to another order in 1903. Then in 1905, the bus business moved from New York to Allentown, Pennsylvania. They also started building trucks using bus chassis with Mack engines. In 1910, the Mack crest trademark was adopted and has been used ever since.

By 1911, Mack Brothers employed over 700 people. By this time, production reached 600 units per year. The operation was known as the International Motor Truck Corporation. In 1916, the AB model was introduced. Also at this time, Mack started building its own components. The AC Mack was also introduced in 1916 and ended production in 1938. The AB model outran the AC in sales totaling over 51,000 units. In 1919, because of the confusion between International Motor and International Harvester, the company directors voted to change the name to Mack Trucks. After World War I, Mack was also building semitrailers.

The AK model, which was similar to the AC, began in 1927. The total production of the AK was 2,819 units. The new B series was introduced in 1928 for long-distance high-speed trucking. The BA, BB, BC, BF, BG, BM, BQ, and BX were in this series with the BQ and the BX being the heavy-duty versions, the largest being the BQ. In the 1930s, the BG, BF, BC, BM, BX, and BQ were matched up with Mack semitrailers. The cab-over-engine design came in 1933 with the CH and CV. The Mack Junior, which was a restyled REO, appeared in 1936. In 1936 the EH model appeared, too, along with the EG, EJ, and EM. The new EQ cab-over-engine model was added to the line.

The year 1940 was the beginning of the famous L series. In 1938, Mack started building its own diesel engines, known as the Lanova diesel. When World War II began, Mack, like other manufacturers, built their share of trucks for military use. Mack produced over 18,000 NO and NR models, which were 6x6s used to haul 155-mm Long Tom field guns. The E series trucks were discontinued, but only to be taken over by the new A series. No L series trucks were built during World War II, but from 1940 to 1953, a total of 12,453 LF, LFT, and LFSW models were built. The heavier version of the L series was the LM and the LJT road tractor. The year 1947 heralded LTLSW, which was the West Coast Mack.

Then in 1953, Mack introduced what would become the most famous of them all, the B model Mack. This series lasted 13 years with a total production of 127,000 units. The B61 model had the biggest production with over 47,000 units, followed by the B42 with over 19,000. The B73 and the B75 replaced the LT model. The H series cab-over-engines came at the same time as the B series and were followed by the G series flat-front cab-over-engine, of which fewer than 2,000 were built. The B series continued into the 1960s, but in 1962 the new F series cab-over made its debut. The C series, R series, and U series all came in the 1960s. In the 1970s, more models were introduced with the Cruiseliner and the Superliner being the more popular. The DM and the Ultraliner were introduced in the 1980s, followed by the CH series and their latest, the new Vision. Mack recently celebrated its 100th anniversary, having earned a name since its beginning in 1901 that has become symbolic of quality and endurance.

The fourth cab-over-engine model in the Mack lineup was the D series. This was the low version that was used mostly for local delivery work. This D-42 was set up as a tractor for the Houston Steel Drum Company of Houston, Texas, in 1955. *Mack Trucks*

The L series was continued into the 1950s. The LH could be spotted by the five-hole Budd wheels. This LH and 32-foot Highway trailer belonged to J. S. Vanderplow Inc. of Muskegon Heights, Michigan. *Mack Trucks Inc.*

The A series started in 1950 and went into 1954. Notice that the fenders were slightly different from those of the L series. Cities Service Oil Company used this A series Mack and Trailmobile tanker to haul gasoline. *Ron Adams Collection*

The appearance of the A series was similar to that of the L series. The American Thread Company purchased this one to pull the Fruehauf Aero-Van trailer. Each series was offering a sleeper cab as an option. *Mack Trucks*

The most-talked-about Mack was the LT model. Though designed for the Western truck operator, they did make their way to the East Coast. C. Rosenbaum Produce and Seafoods was the owner of the LT Mack and Fruehauf reefer trailer. The power source was most likely a 300-horsepower Cummins. The picture was taken in 1958 in the Jersey City area—it was a rather big truck for the East Coast at this time. *Dave Reed*

From 1952 to 1958, Mack offered five cab-over-engine models. The first one was in 1952 with the H-61, known as the "Cherrypicker" because of the high cab. The company or owner is unknown but the picture was taken somewhere in the Los Angeles area. *Stan Holtzman*

Mack's second cab-over-engine model was the W-71 in 1953. Only 215 were made. This was for the Western truck operator. This one was set up as a truck-trailer combination. *Joe Wanchura*

This W-71 was based in the East, leased to the steel division of TransAmerican Freight Lines of Detroit, Michigan. The picture was taken at the old Silver Moon Diner along U.S. 130 in the Pennsauken–Camden, New Jersey, area around 1956. Notice the LJ Mack dump truck on the right side. *Bob Parrish*

Another truck in the Mack line that was designed for the Western operator was the LT, available in several variations. This LT in 1954 was a single-axle designed for pulling Western double trailers such as this set of tankers for Lamb Transportation Company in Long Beach, California. The LT was made from 1947 to 1956 with production at a little over 2,000 units. *Mack Trucks*

The third cab-over-engine Mack was the H-63 in 1954. It was the low version of the H-61. Many of the Eastern trucking companies ran these. This one was leased to North American Van Lines of Ft. Wayne, Indiana, pulling a 1940s Fruehauf Aero-Van furniture trailer. Notice in the showroom window a D model cab-over-engine. *Mack Trucks*

This single-axle model was another version of the H-61 Cherrypicker. The Glidden Quality Products Company hooked it to a Fruehauf Aero-Van reefer to haul those Durkee famous food products. Notice the dual air horns on top of the cab. *Mack Trucks*

The B71 was produced for six years, from 1953 to 1958 with a total of 522. It was powered by a Cummins diesel. Notice how the radiator shell is extended beyond the fenders; the frame had to be extended 6 inches to accommodate the radiator because the Cummins engine was 6 inches longer than the Mack engine. This design was used to keep the engine from going into the cab. Lake Refrigerated Service had this B71 as a sleeper cab. *Neil Sherff*

The numbers in the 80s in the B series were the heavy-duty jobs. This is a 1956 B80 that was owned by the McDonald Petroleum Company. The 80s were mainly the construction and oil field models, but some were used for local deliveries. *Ron Adams Collection*

Chemical Tank Lines of Downingtown, Pennsylvania, owned this H63. The picture was taken in 1957 somewhere in the Camden–Pennsauken, New Jersey, area. Notice the A model sleeper in the background for Harper Motor Lines. *Bob Parrish*

Since their beginning in 1946, the LT was designed to accommodate the Western truck operators. This flatbed truck-trailer combination was Cummins powered and owned by Los-Cal Lumber Company. The horsepower was about 300. *Ron Adams Collection*

Mack manufactured what would become its most famous model, the B, from 1953 into 1966. There were 73 different B models, though some were one-offs, , including busses. This B61 sleeper and produce trailer was owned by Mike Tabbot of Vincennes, Indiana. *Harry Patterson*

Another model was this B61 day cab. The B61 had the highest production in the whole B series with a total of over 47,000 units. E. A. Mariana Asphalt Company of Tampa, Florida, used this B61 to pull one of their asphalt tank trailers. *Ron Adams Collection*

The B73 was another popular model in this series. The B73 and B75 were designed for the Western truck operator. This B73 was owned by I. R. Denny and was used for pulling double Utility cement gondolas. This tractor was powered by a Cummins diesel. *Utility Trailer Co.*

Although the B73 was designed for the Western truck operator, it was also pretty popular with some Eastern truck operators. I. E. Southerland Inc. of Vero Beach, Florida, owned this Cummins-powered B73 Mack and Great Dane stainless steel reefer trailer. These sleepers were known as Charlotte Sleepers. *Neil Sherff*

The fifth cab-over-engine model Mack made was the N series. At first glance, one might have thought it was a C series Ford. The Budd Company made these cabs and sold them to both Ford and Mack. The Holly General Company owned this N model cab-over-engine and Pike drop-floor trailer. Notice the custom-built add-on sleeper compartment. *Ron Adams Collection*

Another same model cab is this N61. This one came without a sleeper. Bill Bauer Trucking of Durand, Wisconsin, was the owner of the tractor and the Wilson livestock trailer. The photo was taken on the plant lot at the Wilson Trailer Company in Sioux City, Iowa. *Wilson Trailer Co.*

Another cab-over-engine that Mack started to produce in 1959 was the G series. Production of these lasted only four years. This is a G75 that was powered by the Mack 673 diesel engine. The tractor and Great Dane reefer trailer were leased to Greenstein Trucking Company of Pompano Beach, Florida. *Neil Sherff*

The H67 was yet another cab-over-engine that Mack produced from 1957 to 1962. This model was similar to the H63 with a little restyling of the fenders and grille. Russell Ruddy of Black Stone, Illinois, had his H67 hooked up to a Wilson cattle trailer. *Neil Sherff*

CHAPTER 12

Peterbilt Motor Company

The end of one company turned into the beginning of another in the case of Peterbilt. After being in the logging business for many years, Al Peterman had to modify his truck fleet to fit his needs. Using the experience he gained, Peterman then purchased the 13-acre West Coast plant of the Fageol company from Sterling in 1939 for $200,000. His goal was to build trucks according to his specifications using the Fageol design, and the first Peterbilt was almost identical to the Fageol.

The Model 260, one of the first Peterbilts made, was a chain-drive logger truck built in 1939. By 1940, production rose to 82 units. The optional engines were Cummins, Waukesha, and Hall-Scott. Most of the early Peterbilts were 6x4 truck tractors and were all the conventional type. To reduce the weight of the trucks, Peterbilt used all aluminum, saving 1,500 pounds over the optional steel construction. In 1944, Peterbilt built 225 trucks for the U.S. government. Also in 1944, the saddening news came that Mr. Peterman had passed of cancer. He didn't live long enough to see his dream turn into a multimillion-dollar operation. After his death, five company employees got together and purchased the company from Ida Peterman for $450,000 in 1946.

In 1948, Peterbilt offered six models that were available in two- and three-axle versions. The complete line of trucks was revised in 1949. Also that same year, Peterbilt acquired the MacDonald Truck and Manufacturing Company. They continued to make a few low-bed trucks, but those faded out three years later. In 1949, Peterbilts sold for $14,000 to $20,000. As the new decade began, the first Peterbilt cab-over-engine was introduced, and company sales grew to $7 million.

Two years later, Peterbilt pioneered the Dromedary truck design. The first such trucks were delivered to Pacific Intermountain Express (PIE). Ringsby Truck Lines also got the Model 451 Dromedary, which was a twin-steer tandem front axle. In 1952, the Model 352 tilt-cab was introduced. Also that year, the nameplate was changed from a rectangle to an oval script. The Models 281 and 351 were built for 11 years after being introduced in 1954. The 281 and 351 cab-over-engine versions were introduced in 1955. The tapered bumper and the skirted fenders gave way to the circular fenders and straight bumper.

In 1958, Pacific Car and Foundry Company (PACCAR) bought the Peterbilt Motor Company. Two years later, the Peterbilt company was relocated to a new $2 million plant in Newark, California. A few changes

were made on the Model 352 COE, including adding quad headlights and a four-piece windshield in 1963. The tilt-hood models arrived in 1965 and the new 359 was introduced in 1967. With sales on the increase, another factory was opened in Madison, Tennessee, in 1969. Available engines included Caterpillar, Continental, Cummins, and Detroit, from a V-6 to a V-12. During the 1960s, the Cummins diesel was the most common engine used by Peterbilt. The total production through the 1960s decade was 21,000 trucks, four times that of the previous decade.

In the early 1970s, Peterbilt introduced their new 110-inch cab-over-engine cab. The three major engines were offered with horsepower from 210 up to 450. By the end of the 1970s Peterbilt was building 9,000 trucks per year, and for that decade more than 72,000 trucks were built. With production on the increase, another factory was built in Denton, Texas. The Newark, California, factory was eventually phased out. As the 1980s came, aerodynamics became the big hit with all the manufacturers, and Peterbilt was no exception.

The year 1989 marked the 50th anniversary of the Peterbilt company. At this time, in celebration, a brand-new Model 379 was given away in a sweepstakes contest. Also, a restored 1939 Model 334TD made a tour of the United States. During the 1990s, Peterbilt struggled to keep its share of the Class 7 and Class 8 market. The company had seven basic models to offer. Through the 1990s, they offered longer-wheelbase trucks and larger sleeper boxes. Air flarings were added to improve aerodynamics. Now, after 60 years, Peterbilt is going strong.

This circa-1951–1952 model Peterbilt truck-trailer combination was owned by Capitol Tank Lines, a California-based tanker hauler. Notice that the turn signals at this time were still the cab-mounted swing-out type. *Ron Adams Collection*

One of the prime freight haulers on the West Coast was West Coast Fast Freight of Seattle, Washington. A mixed bag of equipment, this early-1950s Peterbilt and Fruehauf stainless steel trailer from the 1940s made its runs along the coast. Then in 1955, West Coast became part of the Pacific Intermountain Express operation. Notice that the West Coast graphics were almost identical to those of Watson Brothers Transportation Company of Omaha. *Ron Adams Collection*

Truck number 24, a 1950 Peterbilt, had its work cut out for it on this haul. It's anybody's guess how many board feet there were on this load. The driver looked very proud to drive this truck and the load he was hauling. It looks like the unloading process is about to begin. *Ron Adams Collection*

The picture was taken in 1987 at the ATHS convention in Schaumburg, Illinois. This nicely restored Model 280 Peterbilt got lots of attention. If this long-wheelbase tractor could talk, I'm sure that it would have a few interesting stories to tell of its travels over those Western highways. *Ron Adams Collection*

One of the big Western companies that always experimented with the manufacturers newly engineered trucks was Pacific Intermountain Express of Oakland, California. PIE was a company that tried to use as much of the open vehicle space as they could for extra cargo hauling. The Peterbilt tractor with a Brown Dromedary body and Brown trailer was the way to go. This setup could only be used west of Denver because of the length laws elsewhere. *Brown Trailer Co.*

This nicely restored mid-1950s "Iron nose" Peterbilt was also shot in 1987 at the ATHS convention. Both the previous truck and this truck were owned by the same ATHS member from Kentucky. *Ron Adams Collection*

There was very little chrome on this tractor, which is rather unusual for a Peterbilt. L. Christensen of Seattle, Washington, was the owner of this Peterbilt and Trailmobile rack side trailer. Notice that the tractor has the new oval emblem and the newer narrow bumper. *Joe Wanchura*

This circa-1954 Peterbilt was taking a rest after a long, hard limb. A truck-trailer combination with a day cab was working for the highway garage of Hollister, California. The load was probably palletized. *Brian William*

This driver also pulled into this parking area to cool off his truck from the long, hard pull. The circa-1954 Peterbilt and Utility trailer with a little "Putt-Putt" motor were one of many rigs that did this. *Brian Williams*

In 1952, Peterbilt designed the Model 451 for Ringsby Truck Lines of Denver, Colorado. Ringsby was another company that experimented with trying to make the most of any vacant space on their tractors as they could. This twin-steering job with the sleeper above the cab was their answer. This type of Dromedary rig could not be used east of Denver either, because of length laws. *Ron Adams Collection*

Ringsby Truck Lines had a variety of different equipment in their fleet. Here we see one of their regular over-the-road rigs that were used mostly east of Denver. This mid-1950s Peterbilt Bubblenose cab-over-engine and Fruehauf trailer are climbing a mountain grade somewhere in the Colorado Rockies. *Ringsby Truck Lines*

Another Bubblenose Peterbilt cab-over-engine in the form of a truck trailer was this one owned by Bruns Brothers of Mante, California. It was probably Cummins powered and used for hauling hay, as can be seen. *Brian Williams*

One of the many trucking companies that traveled up and down the Pacific Coast was Los Angeles–Seattle Motor Express (LASME) of Seattle, Washington. Several different makes and types of rigs were in the LASME fleet, one of them being this mid-1950s Bubblenose Peterbilt with day cab and a set of double trailers that look like they could be Trailmobiles. *LASME*

The trucking class of 1955 can be proud of this very sharp-looking 1955 Peterbilt. It is used for hauling hay and is still a working truck today. The chrome extras make this yesterday truck look very good today. *Don MacKenzie*

This style cab-over-engine was the early flat-front tilt-cab. Chertudi Livestock of Caldwell, Idaho, had this truck-trailer combination for hauling livestock. The make of the body and trailer look like they could be a Reliance, Williamsen, or Merritt. *Brian Williams*

Another early-1950s flat-front cab-over-engine Peterbilt Model 352. California-based Camall Services had this one set up as a flatbed Dromedary rig. The neatly stacked load of cargo is unknown. The two gentlemen's names are unknown, but the one on the left is probably the driver and on the right is probably the owner. *Dick Whittington*

PIE of Oakland, California, was a giant Western hauler with several different divisions in their operation. Shown here is a Model 351 Peterbilt that was used in their tank lines division, which covered 11 Western states at this time. Truck-trailer combinations like this one were very popular with tanker operations. *PIE*

The second Model 352 Peterbilt was working in the logging industry. Although this was probably a small load, Peterbilts were capable of hauling much larger loads of logs. The one piece of equipment that all logging trucks had was a cab rack, known as a "headache" rack. *Peterbilt Motor Co.*

This circa-1958–1959 Peterbilt cab-over-engine and Trailmobile double trailers were a common site on the Western highways. The bigger equipment for PIE ran west of Denver and the smaller equipment was used east of Denver. *PIE*

Peterbilt trucks always seemed to get attention because of all the chrome extras that were put on the truck to fancy it up. Russ Phillips Trucking of Fresno, California, went the extra step to make their equipment look nice. *Joe Wanchura*

A Model 281 Peterbilt pulled a set of bottom-dump doubles. Notice where the driver has his spare tire mounted and also the three blue center cab lights. *Ron Adams Collection*

Double trailers not only were pulled by cab-over-engine tractors but by conventional tractors as well. Blincoe Trucking Company of Stockton, California, had this Peterbilt Model 281 hooked up to a set of Utility double flatbed trailers with the outside frame. The cargo could have been some kind of boxed fruit on its way to market. *Brian Williams*

Another truck-trailer combination was this one with a load of finished lumber. The delivery was made by California-based IDACO Lumber Company with a blue-and-white Model 351 Peterbilt that was powered by an 8V-71 Detroit Diesel engine. *Detroit Diesel Division*

C H A P T E R 13
Sterling Trucks

From 1948 to 1951, there was no change in the design of the Sterling trucks. This 1949 Model TA Sterling with propane tank body and pull trailer was owned and operated by Cantlay & Tanzola of Los Angeles, California, a division of Western Truck Lines of the same town. *Cantlay & Tanzola*

William Sternberg started the Sterling company as Sternberg, but changed the name in 1916 because of anti-German sentiments at the beginning of World War I. The trucks Sterling built were 3/4-ton to 7-ton capacity powered by four-cylinder engines. During World War I, Sterling built 489 Class B Liberty trucks. The Hayssen family took over the corporation but kept Ernest M. Sternberg as vice president.

In 1931, Sterling bought the LaFrance Republic Truck Corporation. When the LaFrance Republic parts inventory was depleted, the F series Sterling became LaFrance Republic until 1942. In late 1931, control of the company was taken away from the Hayssen family and Ernest M. Sternberg took over as president. Sterling installed the first diesel engine in a Model FD195H, a Cummins Model H, which became standard equipment. The first Sterling cab-over-engine made its debut in 1934. It was a Model GD967 similar to the F series conventional design. The cab tilted backwards splitting at the top of the windshield. The Shell Petroleum Corporation ordered an unknown number of these cab-over-engine trucks, which were powered by a 100-horsepower Waukesha diesel engine. One variation of the cab-over-engine featured a sleeper over the driver's compartment. Another variation was a four-man cab. In 1937, the entire F series had 17 basic models that used the Waukesha engines. Between 1938 and 1940, 40 percent of the Sterling trucks were powered by the Cummins H series diesel engine. The largest diesel-powered Sterling was set up to pull a full trailer with a GCW of 68,000 pounds. In 1938, Sterling acquired the assets of the Fageol Motor Truck Company through the Waukesha Motor Company. Fageol stopped producing trucks in 1939. The Sterling Company lacked the

capital to purchase the Fageol factory, so the rest of the Fageol business was sold to T. A. Peterman who founded the Peterbilt Motor Company in Oakland, California.

In 1939, the new streamlined I series was introduced, available in both gas and diesel. During World War II, a variety of huge trucks were built for the military. After the war, the H and R series trucks were added to the model line, offered in both gas and diesel. A three-for-one stock split was made in 1946 and Donner Estates of Philadelphia, Pennsylvania, took control of Sterling until the company was sold to the White Motor Company. William G. and Ernest M. Sternberg continued as president and vice president, respectively. In 1947, Ernest M. passed away. The TE and TG series made their debut in 1948. The TE series was the cab-forward design with a short hood. The TG series was the cab-over-engine design, even though it had a short hood. Sterling continued to make chain-drive trucks longer than most other truck manufacturers, but finally discontinued them in 1951.

Between 1948 and 1951, the model line remained unchanged. Then on June 1, 1951, Sterling was bought by the White Motor Company and the two companies became known as Sterling White. In 1952, the Milwaukee operation was shut down and operations were moved to Cleveland. The White Motor Company then bought the Autocar operations in Ardmore, Pennsylvania. Since Sterling and Autocar were the same class trucks, White decided to shut down one of them, so Sterling was discontinued. Some 12,000 Sterling trucks were built over the company's history, with production peaking in the 1920s. The Sterling name disappeared around 1954–1955. Another great truck is gone, but not forgotten.

The Model TE was built from 1950 to 1953. It was Sterling's cab-over-engine model, although it didn't much resemble one. It was offered in both truck and tractor versions. *Sterling*

This is another 1950 Model TE in a tractor version. *Sterling*

Truck-trailer combinations were popular in all makes of trucks. Bob Bryant Livestock Hauling had his 1950 Model TE as a livestock combination. *Joe Wanchura*

Thanks to Einfalt's Scrap Yard of Stockertown, Pennsylvania, this 1950 Model TA was brought back to new life through a beautiful restoration job. *Don MacKenzie*

This 1950 Model HB dump truck hails from Marlboro, Massachusetts, where it was restored. This truck could be one of the last chain-drive trucks that Sterling made. *Ron Adams*

This 1950 Model TA may have come right from the factory in preparation for its first run for Western Truck Lines of Los Angeles, California. Sterlings were popular in this company's fleet, as were Fruehauf trailers. *Western Truck Lines*

S & M Construction Company of Providence, Rhode Island, needed a helping hand to transport its Lorain shovel from one construction site to another. Thanks to Pelso Inc. of Cranston, Rhode Island, the job got done in fine order with the assistance of this 1950 Model HB Sterling and Model TD-75RG-RA Talbert drop-side low-bed trailer. *Talbert Trailers*

In June of 1951, Sterling was purchased by the White Motor Company and the name was changed to Sterling White. This 1951 Model TA was probably one of the first ones made with the new Sterling White emblem. However, notice on this truck that on the radiator top it only appears as Sterling, but on the side of the hood it's wearing the new Sterling White emblem. This one was probably manufactured in the changeover year and to use up any of the old stock parts with the Sterling name on them. Being a tank line hauler, Cantlay & Tanzola of Los Angeles, California, had this truck-trailer set up to haul petroleum. *Cantlay & Tanzola*

Though the new Sterling White emblem appeared on these well-built trucks, the engineering didn't change. K. L. Kellogg and Sons Drilling Company had their 1951 Model TA Sterling White and heavy-duty drop-deck trailer set up to do oil field rigging work. All the necessary equipment is there to do the job.
Ron Adams Collection

This awe-inspiring restoration of a 1952 Model HB by the Forte Brothers was photographed at the American Truck Historical Society Show in Macungie, Pennsylvania, in 1999. *Ron Adams*

Everything shone, including the tires, on this 1951 Model TA Sterling White newly delivered to Western Truck Lines of Los Angeles, California. A Fruehauf stainless steel reefer trailer was coupled to the new tractor. Notice in the background that there is an earlier Sterling and a 1940s-vintage round-nose Fruehauf trailer. *Ron Adams Collection*

With the Gardner heavy-duty low-bed trailer, it is evident that this 1952 Model HB Sterling White was doing lots of heavy-duty-equipment hauling. Note the rugged sheet metal fenders and bumper. It looks like delivery of this truck was on a rainy day, but the dismal weather could not keep these two happy gentlemen from smiling and feeling proud of their new addition. Notice that pickup time was at 11:23 A.M. *Ron Adams Collection*

Reborn again and all dressed up for the show is this 1952 Model HC-20 chain-drive Sterling White dump truck. James W. Flett of Belmont, Massachusetts, is the proud owner of this fine restoration piece. *Dick Copello*

Cement Distributors of Seattle, Washington, had a few 1952 Model TAs in their fleet to haul bulk cement. Sterling White trucks were sold nationwide and several other carriers in the Seattle area used them. *Joe Wanchura*

C H A P T E R　14

White Motor Company

Thomas White started out making sewing machines in Orange, Massachusetts, in 1859, and in 1866 moved his operation to Cleveland, Ohio. After expanding into other manufactured products, White and his four sons—Thomas II, Rollin, Walter, and Windsor—ventured into building their first steam vehicle in 1900. It featured a two-cylinder engine that was mounted under the floor. The White Motor Company was on its way, and by 1906 vehicle production was up to 1,500 units per year.

Early Whites ranged from $2,100 for a 3/4-ton up to $4,700 for a 5-ton model. The company was reorganized in 1916 and had $16 million in capital, which soon increased to $25 million. White built some 18,000 1-ton and 3-ton trucks for World War I. In 1920, the company did almost $52 million in sales. In 1928, a new Model 58 made its appearance. Its carrying capacity was 22,000 pounds to meet the legal weight restrictions in 22 states. At this time, White offered 17 different models, and started making truck tractors with up to 12-ton ratings.

The depression took its toll on some truck manufacturers, allowing White to acquire the Indiana Truck Corporation and then merge with Studebaker, which had acquired Pierce-Arrow. White made its first cab-over-engine in 1935 and used gas engines only through the 1930s. By 1937, they offered 48 different models from 3/4-ton up to the big 10-ton model.

During World War II, White built 20,000 M3A1 scout cars and also 4,000 half-tracks for the military. Trucks and truck tractors were built for the military and were powered by Cummins diesels or Hercules gas engines. In 1949, the 3000 Model White cab-over-engine was introduced. At the start of the 1950s, White absorbed a few more truck manufacturers—Sterling Motor Truck Company in 1951 and Autocar in 1953. The resulting Sterling White trucks were discontinued in 1955 based on the claim that Autocar and Sterling were in the same class. In 1951, an agreement was signed between White and Freightliner to sell Freightliner trucks through White dealerships. The name was then White-Freightliner.

Around 1954, White introduced the Model 9000, as the WC models were still being produced. In 1957, White Motor Company merged with the REO Motor Truck Company, and a year later Diamond T was folded into the White organization. At

this time White came out with the Model 5000 cab-over-engine that was powered by Cummins with 180 to 335 horsepower. Spector Freight System used a few of the 5000 models for the 40-foot turnpike doubles. Clark, Fuller, and Spicer transmissions were offered in the 5000 series. The 1960s brought additional new models such as the 1500 and the 3000. The 1500 was the low-tilt cab-over-engine. The 4000 and 9000 series also came out in the 1960s. In 1967, White merged REO and Diamond T to become known as Diamond REO.

Another newcomer to the White line was the Western Star, designed for the Western trucker. The Road Xpeditor evolved from the Compact in the 1970s. The 7000 series was replaced by the Road Commander with GCW rating at 125,000 pounds. The conventional partner to the Road Commander cab-over-engine was the Road Boss. In 1975 White built the Constructor, their construction vehicle line. In 1977, White's 25-year agreement with Freightliner expired and Freightliner was on its own. A new factory was built in New River Valley, Virginia, to replace the outdated Cleveland, Ohio, plant. In 1981, White was sold to Volvo and became known as Volvo White Truck Corporation. At this time, Western Star became an independent corporation based in Canada. In 1986, GM merged with Volvo and became known as GMC White Volvo. Since then, White has come along with the rest of the manufacturers with their aerodynamic designs. White has come a long way from the first sewing machine in 1859 to today's giant Super Sleeper trucks.

A factory shot of a White WC-24 tractor and Fruehauf trailer. From the appearance of the tractor, it looks like this one may have been going to Roadway Express of Akron, Ohio. *White Motor Co.*

Oil field rigging required special equipment for loading and unloading. Regina Cartage and Storage Company of Regina, Saskatchewan, Canada, made sure their WC28 White was equipped to do the job. The engine was probably a 280 Super Power. *Regina Cartage and Storage Co. Ltd.*

Reefer haulers often made long-distance runs that kept them away from home for days at a time. A sleeper cab was the bedroom away from home. This WC2864 TD White sleeper and Fruehauf reefer were kept busy hauling refrigerated products in the Midwestern states. *Bob Ward*

Another sleeper was this 1951 White WC28 PLTD pulling an American trailer. The same sleeper cab was also offered on other models. *White Motor Co.*

Single-axle sleeper cab tractors were common in the Midwest and eastern states. However, there were also some in the western states. Here we have another White sleeper pulling a set of rack-side doubles taken in southern California. *Stan Holtzman*

Being manufactured in Cleveland, Ohio, Whites were very popular in the Midwest. Bender & Loudon Motor Freight of Akron, Ohio, had a fleet of WC22 Whites. Tractor number 282 is pulling a single-axle Ohio rag-top trailer. *Neil Sherff*

Truck-trailer combinations were a common sight on Western highways. Ohio, Indiana, and Michigan also had truck-trailer combinations. Here we have a White WC-24PLT truck with a pull trailer. Kaplan Trucking Company of Cleveland, Ohio, employed this rig. Steel coils were the load on this trip. *Neil Sherff*

The WC22 Model was very popular with a lot of trucking companies. This owner-operator leased his WC22 sleeper to Daniel Motor Freight of Warren, Ohio, to pull an open-top trailer. *Neil Sherff*

From their beginning Mason-Dixon Lines of Kingsport, Tennessee, was a big user of White trucks. The 1953 White 3000 tractor and Fruehauf Road Star trailer exemplified the kind of equipment that Mason-Dixon Lines ran at this time. In the background is part of their White 3000 fleet. *Mason-Dixon Lines*

White's cab-over-engine was the 3000 series. This is a 1954 302462 PLT model that was owned by Barbara Ann Bread. A Dromedary body fills in the empty space on the long wheelbase. Body and trailer are either Fruehauf or Reliance. Notice the single wheels on the tractor tandem. *Ron Adams Collection*

Sleeper cabs were as popular in the South as they were anywhere. The White WC-22 had a few extra items on it to fancy it up a bit. The Trailmobile trailer has an extra set of mud flaps between the trailer tandem. Southern Fruit and Produce of Richmond, Virginia, felt proud of rig number 86. *Ron Adams Collection*

Middle Atlantic Transportation Company of Bridgeport, Connecticut, had a variety of different trucks in the fleet, including this White 3000 and Fruehauf trailer. This was the new color scheme for the company. Notice how the stack and muffler are also painted blue. During the 1960s they were taken over by Branch Motor Express of New York City. *Middle Atlantic Transportation Co.*

About the biggest White user was and is Roadway Express of Akron, Ohio. This 1955 White 3000 TD and Gindy trailer was one of many in the fleet. The blue-and-orange rigs were a very familiar sight on the highways in the eastern half of the United States. *White Motor Co.*

Another Michigan-type train is this setup put together with two Progress tank trailers. A Model T-50 with capacity of 6,600 gallons on the first trailer and a Model T-30 with capacity of 4,300 gallons on the second trailer was pulled by a White 3000 in the mid-1950s. Farmers Petroleum Co-Op of Lansing, Michigan, was the owner and transporter of the product. *Progress Industries*

These WC-22 Whites were good trucks in their day, but this 1956 WC-22 PLT is still good today along with the 1950 Trailmobile flatbed trailer, thanks to the restoration efforts of Joseph Bowman of Hebron, Ohio. *Dick Copello*

The White 9000 tractor was also a very popular truck with many freight carriers. In this case, Southwest Grease and Oil Company of Wichita, Kansas, also took a liking to the White 9000 Sleeper and the Trailmobile trailer. Dual air horns, dual stacks, and an air conditioner fancy up the rig a little and add some comfort for the driver. *Brian Williams*

Many people were on the move back in the 1950s. North American Van Lines of Fort Wayne, Indiana, was one of the moving companies that was right there to move these people. They had a variety of different makes of tractors and trailers in the fleet. One of those units was this White 3000 and Fruehauf moving trailer. Many of them were sleeper cabs because of the long distances to their destination across the country.
Ron Adams Collection

Many models were offered in several versions, often as optional equipment. This version is in a tandem-axle form with a sleeper cab. This White 4000 model was owned by Dave Howard Grain and Produce of Bowling Green, Kentucky. A Dorsey reefer trailer was used for hauling agricultural commodities. *Neil Sherff*

Through the years, East Texas Motor Freight of Dallas, Texas, was pretty dedicated to using White tractors in their fleet, like this 9000 model. They were seen on the highway of the E.T.M.F. routes that stretched from south Texas to Illinois. A Fruehauf volume van, like this one, was carrying the load. *East Texas Motor Freight*

TransAmerican Freight Lines of Detroit, Michigan, was one of the top-10 trucking companies in the 1950s. One of the tractors in the fleet was a White 5000 Model with a Fruehauf trailer. The 5000 Model was White's first high sleeper cab, introduced in 1959. *Neil Sherff*

White also offered a compact model. Its main purpose was to be used as a city delivery truck, though some were also used as over-the-road tractors. This photo of a White compact and two Fruehauf trailers from the 1940s was taken in the Los Angeles yard of California Cartage Company of Los Angeles, California. *White Motor Co.*

CHAPTER 15

Miscellaneous Trucks of the 1950s

While Kenworth, White-Freightliner, and Peterbilt were the major Western trucks, and while Mack, White, and International claimed the eastern states along with Ford, GMC, and Diamond T, there were other less prevalent makes on the scene in the 1950s as well. Among them were Brown trucks, which were owned by the Associated Transport Company of New York City with the factory in Charlotte, North Carolina. About 1,000 Brown trucks were built in the postwar years. Corbitt was another Southern truck, made in Henderson, North Carolina. Hayes was a Canadian-built truck that was later sold to Mack Trucks and then discontinued in 1976. FWD in Clintonville, Wisconsin, and Oshkosh in Oshkosh, Wisconsin, were builders of similar off-highway and construction trucks. However, both did make some highway tractors. Hendrickson in Lyons, Illinois, made most of their sales in the five-state area around the Great Lakes. They also made a good number of specialty trucks. REOs, Federals, and Studebakers were out there among the rest, trying to keep up with the competition. Other smaller truck builders existed at the time but never made it big. There were those who made only special engineered trucks and trailers, such as Fageol, Cline, Cook Brothers, and LeTourneau, to name a few. Sicard was another Canadian-made truck. Some of the makes, such as Studebaker, Brown, Corbitt, and Federal, ceased production during the 1950s.

Associated Transport Company of New York City owned the Brown Truck and Trailer Company in Charlotte, North Carolina. This restored 1952 Brown, owned by John Long of Burlington, North Carolina, was proudly wearing the graphics of its owner from years ago. *Dick Copello*

This 1951 Brown sleeper was restored by owner Joe Murphy of Grenloch, New Jersey. Notice the tractor number 9069B. The B behind the number meant that this tractor was dispatched out of the Burlington, North Carolina, terminal. *Ron Adams Collection*

The Cline Truck Company started in 1952, in Kansas City, Missouri. The company was mainly an off-highway truck maker but a few were road trucks, such as the one we see here, powered by a Detroit Diesel engine. *Detroit Diesel*

Looking similar to a Freightliner of the 1940s, this early-1950s Brown cab-over-engine tractor was part of the Associated Transport Company fleet, pulling a Brown trailer. *Dave Reed*

The first Corbitt was built in 1910 in Henderson, North Carolina. This turn-of-the-1950s Corbitt was an independent-owner leased to Long Transportation Company of Detroit, Michigan. *Neil Sherff*

This 1950 Model D-802 Corbitt with Cummins diesel power is a very fine-looking restored tractor owned by Steve Rosemond of Hillsborough, North Carolina. *Dick Copello*

Corbitt, like many of the other truck manufacturers, also made sleeper cab versions. The Daniel Company had one to pull this newer Hobbs reefer trailer. The driver has the comfort of an air conditioner in the 1960s (when this photo was taken), which was almost unheard of at the time this tractor was built. *Brian Williams*

This rather unusual-looking cab-over-engine sleeper is a 1951 Model D-603T Corbitt. It was once owned by Turner Transfer Company of Reading, Pennsylvania, and Henderson, North Carolina. The tractor was restored and brought back to life by Donald Smith of Greensboro, North Carolina. The sleeper was in front of the engine and below the floor. *Dick Copello*

Another cab-over-engine of a different style was this Corbitt owned by the Travelift & Engineering Company of Sturgeon Bay, Wisconsin. Notice that the fenders were similar in design to those of the big RD series International. *Neil Sherff*

From 1910 to 1959, Federal trucks were made in Pontiac, Michigan. This 1951–1952-era Federal was owned by Associated Truck Lines of Grand Rapids, Michigan. The tractor had the appearance of a Chevrolet or GMC from the same era. *Neil Sherff*

Clintonville, Wisconsin, was the home and manufacturing place of the FWD trucks since 1910. FWD made lots of trucks for the construction industry but also made over-the-road tractors with five different brand-name engines as the source of power. This mid-1950s FWD and Kentucky reefer were owned by Land O'Lakes Creameries of Minneapolis, Minnesota. *J.B.R. Photographers*

Canadians also manufactured a few trucks of their own. This late-1950s Canadian Hayes was making its way somewhere along the Pacific Coast. Mexi-cana Reefer Service Ltd. of Vancouver, British Columbia, was the company it worked for pulling what looks like it could be a Brown reefer trailer. *Brian Williams*

Hauling construction equipment required specially designed trailers. White Brothers Trucking Company of Wasco, Illinois, had the honors of hauling this 56,000-pound Barber-Green Wheel Ditcher on a Talbert Model T3L-35-FG-T-1 low-bed trailer that is being pulled by a Cummins-powered Hendrickson tractor of early-1950s vintage. *Talbert Trailers*

Here we see Hendrickson's version of their cab-over-engine tractor. Hendrickson used some cabs of other manufacturers for their trucks. This tractor used the RD series International cab. *Joe Wanchura*

The Hendrickson trucks were mainly used in the five-state area around Lake Michigan. This is the R series conventional International cab that was used on a lot of Hendrickson conventional tractors. Wildcat Trucking added some extras to make this tractor look sharp while pulling the Fruehauf four-axle gravel dump trailer. *Neil Sherff*

LeTourneau Inc. of Longview, Texas, built this vehicle known as the "Snowfighter." Designed and built for Alaska Freight Lines of Seattle, Washington, it was capable of transporting 150-ton payloads. It has five 16-x-40-foot cargo beds. The vehicle is 270 feet long running on 24 LeTourneau electric wheels that are 38 inches wide and 88 inches high. The power comes from two sets of diesel electric generating sets each having 400 horsepower with a total of 800 horsepower. The Snowfighter traveled across 1,200 miles of Arctic wasteland into the Arctic Circle, running 24 hours a day at times. *R.G. LeTourneau Inc.*

Midwest Solvents Company of Atchison, Kansas, had its own private fleet of trucks. From left to right: REO, REO, Fageol, KB International, REO, B61 Mack, H63 Mack, Autocar. With Fruehauf, Trailmobile, and Brown trailers, the most unusual one is the Fageol. The photo was taken in 1959. *Ron Adams Collection*

Navajo Freight Lines was one of four major carriers with a home office in Denver, Colorado. Navajo, like many other large Western carriers, had a variety of different makes of trucks and configurations. The first one is a White-Freightliner tractor with a Timpte Dromedary body and trailer. The second one is a 1959–1960 International R West Coaster series and Fruehauf trailer. Both trucks were fully loaded with Festival Queen fresh-tasting strawberry preserves. *Navajo Freight Lines Inc.*

Another private carrier was General Dynamics Corporation This was taken at a California plant. This partial fleet consists of, from left to right: RD Western International, WC White, Model 351 Peterbilt, Model 351 Peterbilt. A van trailer and three tankers of unknown brands were a few in the fleet. *Ron Adams Collection, Steve Rubiolo Photograph*

This mid-1950s fleet belongs to Alterman Transport Lines of Miami, Florida. The partial tractor fleet from left to right is: WC White, LF Mack, B61 Mack, R200 International. All the tractors are sleepers and all four trailers are Great Dane reefers. Alterman was a Florida produce hauler, hauling up to the Midwest and East Coast. *Ron Adams Collection*

This fleet of 12 Internationals, 2 Kenworths, and 1 White-Freightliner belongs to Houck Transport Company of Great Falls, Montana. Houck was a tank lines carrier. Tractor numbers 25, 26, and 22 are the LC 180 to 205 models of the 1952 era. Notice that these three trucks have different style fenders. They are of the square corner construction–type fenders. The International to the extreme right at the end is the Western series. *Houck Transport Co.*

Frank Sibr & Sons of Alsip, Illinois, owned this tank lines fleet consisting of two different models of Hendrickson and one B61 Mack. The trailers are all Heil gasoline tankers. The Hendrickson tractor to the extreme far right looks like it could be an earlier model than the rest. *Frank Sibr & Sons Inc.*

Five different makes of trucks make up this fleet and they are as follows from left to right: mid-1950s Chevrolet, straight-truck-era Fords, DC100 Autocar, RD West Coaster International, Kenworth. Hauling pipes seems to be the business for this unknown company. *Van Guard Photography*

Found in someone's junkyard is this 1949–1950 W series Oshkosh. This Oshkosh, along with several other makes, was located outside Phoenix, Arizona. Oshkosh trucks were mainly specialty trucks made for heavy hauling and the construction industry, although some over-the-road tractors did exist. *Don MacKenzie*

Another early-1950s REO sleeper cab, this one diesel powered and most likely a Cummins. The company was Trans-Cold Express of Dallas, Texas, as it was around this time when Trans-Cold was starting out in the refrigerated hauling business. *Joe Wanchura*

In 1955, REO redesigned their truck line. The grille styling went from pointed to a flat grille. As can be seen, it is diesel powered and probably a Cummins. *Neil Sherff*

In 1955 REO introduced their cab-over-engine. Signal Trucking Service of Los Angeles, California, had at least one pulling a set of Utility doubles. Signal operated between Los Angeles and the San Francisco Bay area with a variety of equipment. *Signal Trucking Service*

This restoration, owned by Chuck Gamber of Ellicott City, Maryland, is a 1959 A-632 REO. The famous Gold Comet engine powered this truck. *Dick Copello*

In 1902 the first Studebaker truck was built. This early-1950s tractor was one of many that were made over Studebaker's 62-year history. The trailer is a late-1940s Fruehauf Aero-Van. The picture was taken in 1955 at Flint, Michigan. *Neil Sherff*

The Sicard was a Canadian make. They did manufacture over-the-road tractors, but this was a 1957 15 Model T-273 C dump truck. *Ron Adams Collection*

Over the years, there were many specially designed trucks that were a little strange looking, but each one had a purpose. This tractor, possibly an International, had its work cut out for it to move the huge generator. There is another source of power in the rear to push the 16-wheel low-bed trailer and its load to its destination. Southwestern Transfer Company of El Paso, Texas, was tapped to do the job. *Ron Adams Collection*

Index

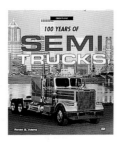

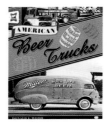
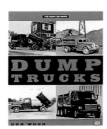
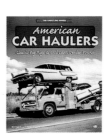

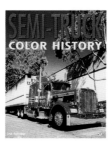